Reinventing the Family

REINVENTING THE FAMILY

IN SEARCH OF NEW LIFESTYLES

ELISABETH BECK-GERNSHEIM

Translated by Patrick Camiller

polity

This edition © Polity Press, 2002. First published as Elisabeth
Beck-Gernsheim, *Was kommt nach der Familie?* © C.H. Beck'sche
Verlagsbuchhandlung, München, 1998.

First published in 2002 by Polity Press in association with Blackwell
Publishers Ltd
Published with the assistance of Inter Nationes, Bonn.

Editorial office:
Polity
65 Bridge Street
Cambridge CB2 1UR, UK

Marketing and production:
Blackwell Publishers Ltd
108 Cowley Road
Oxford OX4 1JF, UK

Published in the USA by
Blackwell Publishers Inc.
350 Main Street
Malden, MA 02148, USA

ISBN 0-7456-2213-5
ISBN 0-7456-2214-3 (pbk)

A catalogue record for this book is available from the British Library and has
been applied for from the Library of Congress.

Typeset in 11 on 13 pt Berling
by Kolam Information Services Private Limited, Pondicherry, India
Printed in Great Britain by MPG Books Ltd, Bodmin, Cornwall

This book is printed on acid-free paper.

Contents

Contents

Preface to the English Edition

Of all the changes shaking the world today, none is more important to us than those which affect the core of our personal life – sexuality, love and marriage, relationships and parenthood, the various personal networks with which we actively identify. Here, the revolution that has been transforming the foundations and models of everyday life is apparent not least in the resistance that constantly forms against it. In many parts of the world we can witness heated debates about 'gender equality', 'women's rights' and 'the future of the family'. In fact, the word 'debates' is rather misleading; it plays down the fact that they sometimes involve warlike hostilities fought out with fundamentalist zeal. What are the changes that trigger such turbulent reactions? Which cultural circles are affected by them? Let us just mention a few of the key points that will be developed more systematically in various chapters of this book.

- The pre-industrial family was a community centred upon work and economics.
- One of its crucial features was the inequality between husband and wife, including matters relating to their sexual life, where double standards also served to support established norms on the ownership and inheritance of property.

- Women and children had scarcely any rights of their own.
- Homosexuality was considered 'unnatural' and treated as a perversion.

Since those times, the basic terms on which people cohabit or lead their lives together have dramatically changed.

- Modern medicine has increasingly provided the means for sexuality and reproduction to be separated from each other. A field of sexual experimentation has thus opened up, together with newly differentiated types of biological and social parenthood.
- Since the 1960s, women in many Western countries have achieved equality with men in education or even partly overtaken them, and female participation in paid employment has also increased, though by no means in the same proportions. As a result, the family has more and more been losing its significance as an economic community.
- Whereas material interests used to be the decisive factor, romantic love is now the basic premise guiding how people approach marriage.
- One important consequence of this is the huge increase in divorce-rates that has occurred in a number of countries.
- In the industrially developed countries, fewer and fewer people live within the kind of family that used to be considered 'normal' in the 1950s – that is, a unit involving an officially sanctioned lifelong bond between an economically active husband and an economically inactive wife and the children they have together.
- Same-sex relationships still experience widespread discrimination, but they are acquiring greater social, legal and official recognition.

All this has led to the coexistence of multiple forms of family life. If the hippie motto 'Let a hundred flowers bloom' applies anywhere, then it must be here in the growing diversity of 'post-familial families'.

The theory of individualization

As the family landscape has grown more complex, the research field too has become ever more specialized. In this twofold context, the unity of the concept of the family has itself been called into question. This book will present a medium-range theory – *the theory of individualization* – that enables us to combine several different theoretical as well as empirical and historical references (Beck and Beck-Gernsheim 2001).

When we speak of 'individualization', we always have a two-fold tendency in mind. On the one hand, the traditional social relationships, bonds and belief systems that used to determine people's lives in the narrowest detail have been losing more and more of their meaning. From family unit and village community through region and religion to class, corporation and gender role, what used to provide a framework and rules for people's daily lives has become increasingly brittle. New space and new options have thereby opened up for individuals. Now men and women can and should, may and must, decide for themselves how to shape their lives – within certain limits, at least.

On the other hand, individualization means that people are linked into the institutions of the labour market and welfare state, educational system, legal system, state bureaucracy, and so on, which have emerged together with modern society. These institutions produce various regulations – demands, instructions, entitlements – that are typically addressed to individuals rather than the family as a whole. And the crucial feature of these new regulations is that they enjoin the individual to lead a life of his or her own beyond any ties to the family or other groups – or sometimes even to shake off such ties and to act without referring to them. Talcott Parsons called this 'institutionalized individualism', a structural phenomenon guiding and shaping people's lives in modern Western societies.[1] Individuals must learn to cope with the sets of regulations that come into force under conditions of institutionalized individualism. Otherwise they have to take the consequences – and the blame. For it is central to the creed of the new institutions that they demand and promote people's active steering of their own lives. In the education system and even more in the labour market, the principle is: Go your own way! Move forward, never stand still! The only way to succeed is by asserting yourself!

There is just one small yet crucial question. What happens when this individualization spiral keeps piling up the pressure and the incentive to lead 'a life of one's own' – what happens then to the family?

What 'flexibilization' and 'deregulation' entail

Let us take Britain, for example, where the forms of private life have been changing especially fast. 'In the space of one generation', according to a report by the Office of National Statistics, 'the numbers marrying have halved while the numbers divorcing have trebled and the proportion of children born outside marriage has quadrupled.' [2] There is growing concern among politicians and the public at large about these trends. The Labour Government – with Tony Blair himself to the fore – has championed a new emphasis on the family, celebrating 'family values' as a means of salvation rather than a synonym for tedium and narrow-mindedness. We need parental upbringing, it is said, and we need a new marriage culture so that couples learn to live with each other and to form more dependable ties. In the labour market, attempts must be made to bring about a change of consciousness so that it becomes easier to combine a job and a family.

Unfortunately, however, few concrete measures have so far been on offer. This is hardly surprising. For so long as one remains at the level of values, culture and consciousness, there is no need to grapple with the reality of a competitive labour market which, especially in Britain, is becoming ever more insecure and unequal; nor any need to consider how the much-touted family values relate to New Labour's own preachings on 'flexibilization' and 'deregulation' of work. Everyone is supposed to be their own little entrepreneur, ever on call, ever ready to work. Just keep at it and you will be rewarded!

This is the contradiction in which New Labour has trapped itself (Franks 1999: 210 ff). On the one hand, it wants to train everyone in self-assertion and personal initiative and to keep increasing the demands on labour; on the other hand, it seeks to conjure up a new marriage culture and expects people to be more family-conscious and willing to have children. The two do not add up. So New Labour of all parties forgets what the labour market looks like and what flexibilization and deregulation entail in private life. Not only children but also couples suffer when work stretches further and further round the clock and round the globe. Seven-day weeks and twenty-four-hour days, shift work and irregular changes in working hours, training courses in different cities, weekend seminars, business trips, evening meetings: such a rhythm can be tolerated if you are still young and healthy and single. But two of you? How long can duty rosters be matched to each one's whereabouts? When will it all become too much of an effort? Who will find it too gruelling to take? How many relationships eventually crack under the strain?

It is true that flexibilization has been carried further in Britain than in other European countries, but the basic conflict is generally much the same. And because no simple solution is in sight, politicians elsewhere also do not want to know the uncomfortable truth that the abilities, attitudes and actions demanded by the new labour market do not make people fitter for a life of close and dependable long-term relationships. At work, more market, more competition, more speed, more change; in personal life, more community, more conciliation, more patience and more consideration for others. How is that supposed to happen?

The new relationship of tension

The chapters that follow do not have any patent cures to offer. But possibly – hopefully – they may contribute to a more precise analysis and to a clearer picture of the forces expressed in present-day relations between the sexes and the generations. What drives people to search for new ways of living, and what hopes are associated with that search? What are the possible solutions, the demands and the constraints which they encounter along the way? And when people today are pulled by different, incompatible expectations, what are the resulting uncertainties and conflicts between men and women, between children and parents, and in relations between the old and the young? How might things shape up in the future? Such will be the questions running through this book.

Acknowledgements

Crown copyright © material is reproduced under HMSO Class Licence C01W283 with the permission of the Controller of HMSO.

1

The New Confusion about the Family

In Western industrialized societies, songs of praise were regularly sung to the family during the 1950s and 1960s. In West Germany it was enshrined in the constitution and given special state protection; it was the recognized model for everyday life, and the dominant sociological theory regarded it as essential to a functioning state and society. Then came the late sixties and early seventies, when the revolt of the student and women's movements against traditional structures exposed the family as ideology and prison, as site of everyday violence and repression. But then another counter-shift brought to the fore voices calling for 'defence of the bourgeois family' (Berger and Berger 1984) as a 'haven in a heartless world' (Lasch 1977). A 'war over the family' broke out (Berger and Berger 1983). Suddenly it was no longer even clear who or what constituted the family. Which types of relationship should be described as a family and which should not? Which are normal, which deviant? Which ought to be encouraged by the state and receive financial support?

Meanwhile, at the beginning of the twenty-first century, the situation has become even more confused. Instead of the wild slogans of the early seventies, a new crusade – especially in the United States, but to some extent also in Britain and Germany – is developing in the name of 'family values' (see the Preface; and also, for example, Stacey 1995). It would be wrong to conclude from this that the clock is simply being turned back, since the fundamentalist rhetoric concerning the family is more in the way of a reaction than of an actual return to older forms and standards. As various surveys have shown, some groups in society do retain a traditional image of the family, but others have turned resolutely against it and most display a contradictory mixture of traditional ideals and new expectations distributed in different ways according to gender and generation. The ensuing landscape of hopes and disappointments has given rise to a wide variety of ways of living, loving and forming relationships – welcomed by some, endured by others, but also bitterly resisted by many. The result of all these changes is that, in politics, academic research and everyday life, it is no longer clear who or what is part of the family. The boundaries are becoming unclear, the definitions uncertain. There is a growing loss of security.

The concepts no longer apply

This being so, it is difficult even to speak of the family. For many of the familiar concepts no longer apply: they sound outdated, perhaps even a little suspicious; many of them can no longer catch the ways in which young people live and think about their lives. If we take the example of 'marriage', one of the main concepts in question, it is obviously not enough to focus on a paper certificate. In work, leisure and the routine of everyday life, even in official forms and invitation cards, the references are increasingly to 'couples', 'partnerships' or 'relationships'. The tendency is toward 'life companions' or even, in one ironic expression, to 'part-life companions'.

Official statistics still use the term 'single people'. But it would be wrong to think they always live alone. Some of those who count as 'single' live with others in a communal household. Others have a stable relationship with someone, without sharing a household. In this common form of city life, 'a single household and single status do not mean the foregoing of a relationship, but only that two people have not chosen the form of married life and prefer "living apart together"' (Bertram 1994: 23). This example shows the emer-

2

gence of finely differentiated lifestyles for which no room is provided in our usual categories (in this case, official household statistics). And any attempt to force these new forms into the old containers would inevitably falsify the reality.

Things become even more complicated when children are brought into the picture. In bourgeois society the model was a lifelong father–mother–child unit, legitimated by the registry office. In deviant cases one spoke of a 'single mother' or 'unmarried mother', always with the implication that she had been deserted by the man; a disreputable, 'fallen' condition, somewhere between exploitation and rejection. Nowadays, however, we have the respectable category of the 'single parent', which exists even in upper-middle-class circles. It includes women who used to be married, have subsequently divorced, and are now bringing up one or more children alone; women who have never been married and have brought up their child or children alone from the start (perhaps because they planned it like that, or because their relationship with a partner broke down before the child was born); and women who count as 'single parents' in the official statistics but who share their home and everyday life with the child's father without having obtained a marriage certificate. Nor does this by any means complete the list. There are also, for example, widowed mothers, male single parents, and homosexual partners with children.

Thanks to the advances of medical technology and the various modes of artificial insemination, the very concept of 'parenthood' (fatherhood, motherhood) has become unclear. Whereas it used to be the case that *pater semper incertus*, that no one could say for sure who was the father of a child, now this can be conclusively demonstrated through a simple genetic test. On the other hand, we now have the sperm donor who is nothing other than a progenitor (and even that only by a technological detour), who often has not even met the mother – not to speak of having physical contact with her. At the same time, the *mater* herself has to some extent become *incerta*, as one sees in the case of the surrogate mother who, in return for payment, may have been artificially inseminated and gone though a pregnancy for an unknown couple desperate to have a child of their own. (Sometimes, though, they may all end up in court before a judge arguing over who is the child's 'real' mother.) Or take the case of the older, post-menopausal woman who becomes pregnant by having an embryo implanted from a younger woman (so that the child she bears is not biologically her own). All kinds of other, less-known variants may be found in the medical literature. But the most important point here is that, through the new operations of medical technology, forms of parenthood are becoming possible which have never before existed or even been conceivable. Biological and social parenthood are thus being separated from each other and fused together in novel combinations.

The confusion of names

In addition to the rapid development of medical technology, changes in family law have created various new options. With regard to names, for instance, the family name was once a visible sign to the outside world of who belonged to the family. Today, in a London school, there is a six-year-old boy who has no surname. He used to have one – or, rather, two; for his parents, who lived together for many years without ever marrying, decided officially to give their three children two surnames. As this was a little awkward, the parents agreed that for everyday purposes the two girls would bear their mother's name and the boy his father's name. But when the couple subsequently split up, in not very harmonious circumstances, the mother went along to the school to get the son's name changed. The father learnt of this only when the son showed him the end-of-term report. He then went himself to the school and demanded that the name be changed once more. The school administration agreed to this, but at the same time explained that it would again have to give its consent if the mother came back and demanded a further name change. The case has now been referred to the local authorities, and pending their decision the boy's exercise books and personal locker carry only his first name.[1]

This is admittedly a rather exotic case, and it would not have been possible under German law. Nevertheless, in Germany too new legislation has led to some interesting name changes. The times are gone when Section 1355 of the Civil Code could baldly state that 'the wife bears her husband's surname' and thereby also determine the children's name. Since 1977 new forms and combinations have gradually become possible, supplemented by regulations covering a fixed period of transition. A couple may now opt for a common surname (either the husband's or the wife's) or one partner may adopt a double name; both may revert at any point to the name of their birth and renounce their former partner's name; or they may, after years of living together, decide to adopt a common name. Both in Britain and Germany: 'Now that fewer women change their names when they marry and/or get divorced and/or have children by more than one man outside marriage, a family name no longer denotes a family.'[2]

In practice this often creates confusion, since the old expectations persist at many levels of everyday life:

> The woman on the first floor simply can't make it out. After more than two years, she still says 'Herr Galal' to Bernhard Hammes. She often meets his wife – that is, Frau Galal – in the hall and she has taken note of their names. But she can't make head nor tail of the newfangled regulations. Shadea Galal and Bernhard Hammes have been married since 1991, yet they have kept their surnames. For Shadea Galal it was not just a question of the sublime sound of her Egyptian name; she also sees it as part of her identity.

But, where such a choice is made to keep separate names, everyday life becomes full of little nuisances: wrongly addressed letters; invitations to a non-existent Frau Hammes, Hammes-Galal or Galal-Hammes. It also becomes more difficult to complete forms, which, as in the case of tax returns, may have no place for the wife's own name. Things really hot up with the birth of a child. 'At the kindergarten or school and in the local neighbourhood, anyone who does not have the same name as the child is not treated as the father or mother unless they have positive proof. Or the offspring count as born out of wedlock.'[3]

Much ado about nothing?

The newly available name combinations are regarded by many as a pointless and impractical fashion that is more trouble than it is worth, 'because you can no longer tell who belong together and how'. This is a superficial view of things, however, which fails to grasp the deeper changes expressed in the outward signs. When Anna Kahn marries Walter Gruhl but wants to continue being called Kahn, this is symptomatic of a wider demand by women for 'a bit of a life of their own' (see Beck-Gernsheim 1983; Beck et al. 1995). Or, to put it in more general, more gender-neutral terms, the decision of a married couple to keep different names is symptomatic of the demand for autonomy which is nowadays (not always, but more and more) considered valid and reciprocally exercised within relationships – symptomatic, that is, of the emphasis on a biography, roots and identity of one's own, of the claim to a bit of a life of one's own within a life *à deux*. Here too, though neither expressed nor agreed, the lesson that marriage vows are not a long-term guarantee – that, however much one wishes it, the partnership will not necessarily last for life – must also play a significant role. This implies that it may be wiser, or anyway more prudent, not to adopt a new name which might one day be the cause of all sorts of trouble – whether because it has to be given up again, or because it means carrying around the memory of one's ex-partner.

Just as the names of family members are not empty words but bear within them a history of social change (of gender relations, for example), so are the relationships dealt with by researchers and policy-makers in the field of the family anything but insignificant. They too are markers of a change that has been taking place – and especially of the controversies that surround it. It is not an arbitrary matter, or academic hairsplitting, whether one speaks of 'family' in the singular or 'families' in the plural,[4] or whether the concept of the family is abandoned and stealthily replaced with others such as 'family lifestyles' or simply 'lifestyles'.[5] What are involved, rather, are a number of hotly contested issues. Should we stick to – and consider as correct, normal and appropriate – the traditional image of the family as a lifelong father–mother–child unit legitimated by the registry office? Should we regard other forms as incomplete and deviant, deficient and dysfunctional? Or, on the contrary, should the claims to precedence of the traditional form be rejected? Should more attention be paid to all the lifestyles and types of relationship that are developing outside what has traditionally counted as a normal family? And where these forms assertively demand recognition and equal consideration – for example, in the law of inheritance, in fiscal regulations or other dealings with public authorities – should their claims be granted? More specifically, to turn again to the case of medical technology, should the possibilities of artificial insemination be open only to married women, on the grounds that marriage still offers the best protection for the child's welfare? Or should they be available to anyone who so wishes – including unmarried and homosexual couples or women without a partner – on the grounds that the child's need will be for care and affection, not an official rubber stamp? Or is the idea to uphold in principle the right of the most diverse lifestyles to exist, but to require, in the name of the child's welfare (defined how?), at least a stable partnership for the application of medical technology to planned parenthood?

The contours of the post-familial family

We are now at the heart of a topic that the following chapters will address from different angles and with different emphases. The key question, to outline it in advance, is what happens when the old certainties (rooted in religion, tradition, biology, etc.) lose much of their force without actually disappearing and new options redraw the areas for personal choice, not in a free space outside society but in one that involves new social regulations, pressures and controls. Or, in sociological terms, how does the individualization drive of the last few decades enter ever more strongly into the area of the family, marriage and parenthood, effecting a lasting change in relations between the sexes and the generations? How, under the conditions of individualization, does a historically new tension arise which, though certainly not making relationships simpler, perhaps makes them more stimulating and appealing?

So, how does this leave the provocative question: what comes next after the family? It is often thought that those who speak of individualization have in mind a straightforward end to the family and the emergence of a 'singles society' (e.g. Hradil 1995a: 82 ff). But this is a misunderstanding – and not a minor one at that. The picture that the following chapters will try to draw is not so simple or one-dimensional. For processes of individualization generate *both* a claim to a life of one's own *and* a longing for ties, closeness and community. The answer to the question 'What next after the family?' is thus quite simple: the family! Only different, more, better: the negotiated family, the alternating family, the multiple family, new arrangements after divorce, remarriage, divorce again, new assortments from you, my, our children, our past and present families. It will be the expansion of the nuclear family and its extension over time; it will be the alliance between individuals that it represents; and it will be glorified largely because it represents an image of refuge in the chilly environment of our affluent, impersonal, uncertain society, which has been stripped of its traditions and exposed to all kinds of risk (Beck and Beck-Gernsheim 1995: 2).

Thus, it would be a misunderstanding to conclude that people become so egoistic and hedonistic that they live only in accordance with their own needs, and that unstable, even wildly unstable, relationships spread on all sides. What is to be expected is that for most people stable periods will alternate with others (before, alongside or after marriage, with or without a certificate) when they play, juggle and experiment with relationships, partly because they choose to do so, partly because they are more or less forced into it. And, please note, it is nowadays also to be expected that, even in the ordinary course of stable relationships, far more questions requiring a conscious decision may arise – whether because such options previously did not exist at all or only in exceptional cases, or because the binding assumptions of old have largely broken down – and that the resulting conflicts will often gain a momentum and drama of their own which catch the participants unawares. Let us look at a few hardly exotic questions from everyday life. They are ones to which we shall return.

Should we move in together, or should we at first (or perhaps for a longer time) keep our own apartments? Should we have children straightaway or later on or perhaps never, or should we keep our options open? If children do not come in the natural course of things, should we try artificial insemination or something else from the range of what medicine has to offer? If one of us gets a secure and well-paid job in another town, should the family move there or should we try commuting and a weekend marriage? Who will then look after the kids during school holidays? What do we do in the case of illness? And what if even granny goes away? If our parents-in-law need more help on a daily basis or grandad becomes in permanent need of nursing, who will take care of them? If my husband has left me or I him, and we both live in new relationships, should I go on inviting my former parents-in-law to the children's birthday? If my partner is a foreigner, should we stay here for good or one day go to his or her native country? Should the children be brought up speaking two languages and holding dual citizenship? What identity do we want to convey to them?

This catalogue of questions, which mirrors the hopes and disappointments, the opportunities and terrors of living under conditions of individualization, displays a subversive power in everyday life, and often enough a silent, dogged rancour. What it shows most clearly is that less and less is given once and for all in people's lives; that more and more often new starts must be made and new decisions taken. Where the dynamic of individualization imposes itself, more effort than before must be expended to keep the various individual biographies within the ordinary compass of the family. How much drama and diplomacy is involved! Whereas one used to be able to fall back upon well-adapted rules and rituals, we now see a kind of stage-management of everyday life, an acrobatics of discussion and finely balanced agreement. When this is unsuccessful, the family tie becomes fragile and threatens to collapse. People do still live within relationships, but these are different from before in terms of scope, obligation and duration.

This does not mean that the traditional family is actually vanishing, but it is clearly losing the monopoly that it for so long enjoyed. Its quantitative significance is declining with the spread of new lifestyles which do not usually aim at living alone but seek ties of a different kind: for example, cohabitation without a marriage certificate or without children; a single-parent family, 'conjugal succession' or a same-sex partnership; weekend relationships and part-life companionship; living in more than one household or between different towns. So, more and more intermediate forms, before, alongside and after the family, are appearing on the scene: these are the contours of the 'post-familial family'.

The variety of family forms in earlier times

It may be asked what is so new or exciting about this diagnosis.[6] In previous centuries there were certainly various forms of the family, not just one uniform type: the history books tell of kings, princes and dukes who had a 'marriage on the side', keeping an official mistress and showering their illegitimate offspring with titles and possessions. Studies from social history show that as early as the nineteenth century many regions had a high proportion of births out of wedlock, sometimes even higher than today. And, if one looks at old church registers and family albums, one finds a large number of second or third marriages and all manner of step-relatives:

> Let us take as an example the Frankfurt merchant Peter Anton Brentano, born in 1735. His first marriage was with a cousin, who bore him six children and died in 1770. Three years later he married a second time, to the 17-year-old Maximiliane von La Roche (twenty-one years younger than himself). She brought twelve children into the world during the twenty years they were married, then died in 1793 at the age of 37. Brentano subsequently took a third wife, again much younger, and before his death in 1797 he produced with her another two children. A

similar but little-known case is that of the 27-year-old merchant Johann Peter Müllensiefen, who in 1756 married a landowner's daughter Anna Elisabeth Heuser. She died in 1763 after bearing three children, and a year later he wedded Anna Maria Birkenbach, who in turn passed on in 1770 after the birth of two children. Two years later, he married a third time and had another two children with his new spouse. His son from the second marriage – Peter Eberhard, born in 1766 – limited himself to two marriages: the first, in 1794, lasted only three years before Frau Minna died in her first childbirth; five months later the widower married again. His second wife, twelve years younger than himself, died at the age of 37 shortly after the birth of her ninth child. Müllensiefen, by now 48, did not enter into another marriage. (Frevert 1996: 5)

How much changing around, how much confusion even in those days! Fascinated by the sequence of abruptly ending and immediately resuming marriage, one glimpses only in passing what constitutes the difference and where the historical analogy has its limits. In earlier centuries the high number of successive marriages and families was caused by the high mortality, whereas today it is a result of high divorce-rates; then an external stroke of fate, now a deliberate act involving a decision of one's own (or at least of one's partner). This is not a casual difference – on the contrary. At the level of personal experience, the partner's death did bring feelings of loss, mourning and pain, but not that peculiar emotional bitterness, with its mutual recrimination and wounding but also inner feelings of guilt and failure, which often accompanies divorce; nor any post-marital disputes over custody, alimony or the division of property held in common, those typical elements which, from the social-structural point of view, involve an independent dynamic and drive the spiral of individualization onward (see chapter 2). Moreover, the successive families of old did not involve any offence against what was deemed right and proper; indeed, they literally corresponded to the ideal of 'till death do us part'. Today, however, successive families are a sign that the ideal is crumbling. When every third marriage ends in a divorce court, or even more in the case of some other Western countries, no one can seriously claim that lifelong marriage is a generally recognized and generally respected institution. The old ideal has gradually been replaced by a new one along the lines of 'So long as things are going well'. In other words, we stay together for as long as we want to – which, if only implicitly, keeps life open for new options, new attractions and ties.

And then there were the great and the mighty! Without wishing to go here into the history of their mistresses, concubines and playmates, we may consider it historically proven that, in this respect too, many were used to a lavish lifestyle. At least in times when their power was at its greatest, they could take many a liberty that was not allowed to their subjects – in sexual matters as in other areas of life. No one could dare to cross them, and anyone who did lived dangerously indeed. Take, for example, Henry VIII and his six wives. In order to get his way, he organized the execution of one of the spouses of whom he had tired and even founded a new state church into the bargain – not the least of its purposes being to make divorce a possibility. Obviously such courses of action were not open to everyone. And, when the times became more democratic, even the rulers had increasingly to bow to the prevailing precepts. Take Edward VIII, for example, a twentieth-century successor of Henry VIII. In the 1930s, when he lost his heart to the divorcee Mrs Simpson and wanted to make her his legitimate spouse, he was forced to give up the throne. The poor man – if only he had lived a little later! For by the end of the twentieth century the amorous adventures and marital dramas of the British royals were the daily fare of the tabloid gossip columns. This does not mean that the rulers live by laws of their own – but, on the contrary, that the old models are crumbling in a quite democratic way, from top to bottom of society. In a country like Britain, where today some 45 per cent of marriages end in divorce, the turbulent family sagas of various members of the royal family are not exceptions but part of the general trend. And what's the point of marrying, the divorced Charles now seems to ask, as he gives his heart but not his hand to the divorced Camilla. His great-uncle Edward had been neither able nor willing to get involved in such distinctions.

The rise and fall of a model of the family

The historical examples in the last section show us only discrete parts; they do not afford a full picture of 'the' family across different epochs, regions and sections of the population. But at least they give some sense of the fact that the family form which we know for short as 'traditional' does not at all go back to the beginning of human history, and that it is therefore not the only one to be 'natural' or 'proper'. In fact, as various historical studies have shown, it is a form which emerged quite late in the day, partly under the influence of Christianity and its teachings, and essentially with the transition from pre-industrial to industrial society, the change in the family from a working unit to an economic unit, and the rise of the bourgeoisie in the course of the eighteenth and nineteenth centuries. These were the conditions in which the model of the 'traditional' family – a lifelong officially legitimated community of father–mother–child, held together through emotion and intimacy – reached its highest form and began to spread far and wide, even if it initially had to overcome various kinds of resistance.

Let us now take as a final historical example those regions for which the nineteenth-century population statistics show a high rate of births out of wedlock. Should we conclude that morals there were more permissive, or even that 'illicit' relations were the rule? Anyone who thinks so will be disappointed. For the social background described in the historical studies makes it clear that the relations in question were structured, lasting and socially recognized. The obstacles in the way of an official wedding were external ones: the inheritance rules for peasants and the ban on marriage for those without property of their own. Thus we read in one study of births outside marriage in Austria:

> this attitude to household service was the main reason why marriage did not occur. For it is customary on the land that the son or daughter serves as a farmhand on the father's or another person's farm, and that the son marries only when he has inherited the property from his father. The son and his

intended must therefore often wait for years before entering into marriage. (Hecke, quoted in Haslinger 1982: 9)

'His intended': this formula already shows the basic intention. People wanted to marry, but were unable to do so before the farm was handed down. The strength of marriage as a norm in the nineteenth century, however, may be seen precisely in the fact that the battles over family law were battles for and over marriage, or rather for new regulations that would make a 'legitimate' tie available to people in all property categories and classes (Blasius 1992: 82). This is exactly what has changed. Today, at the beginning of the twenty-first century, the external obstacles to marriage have long been overcome – yet more and more couples live together without marrying, and quite a lot keep this up even when they have children. They do this not because of the external pressure of circumstances, but through a voluntary decision of their own. They can no longer see any point, or any need, to have their alliance rubber-stamped by officialdom.

Let us sum up the lessons of the historical material. It is true that in former times, too, there were various patterns and not just one uniform family type. But, whereas the variety then used to depend mainly upon external circumstances, it today depends mostly upon people's own decisions. Those who do not live in accordance with the model of the so-called normal family often do so because the old judgements of what is 'normal' or 'deviant' no longer make sense to them; or perhaps also because they have given it a try and found that they could not keep it up. More pointedly, we might say that whereas there used to be many exceptions but also impressively solid rules it is now in many respects no longer clear what is the exception and what is the rule – especially as it is also unclear where people can find any guidance for the new questions and decisions that confront them, in a globalizing world marked by scientific and technological change, labour-market risks and other tendencies which spill over into the realm of the private.

In short, for quite a lot of the middle and older generation, and even more for the younger generation, the landscape of family life has opened up and the ground has become unstable. An ever greater number of people cobble together a lifestyle of their own from bits and pieces of assorted hopes, sometimes with and sometimes without success. This is the raw material from which the new variety is formed.

2

When Divorce Becomes Normal

Divorce is occurring at a brisk pace.

Josef Schmid (demographer)

In times when marriage is an irrevocable decision, even a divorce has something monotonous about it. It enjoys a popularity that can make you feel sick.

Wolf Wondratschek (writer)

Andrew J. Cherlin, one of the best-known family researchers in the United States, published a book in 1981 with the title *Marriage, Divorce, Remarriage*. In the preface to a new edition that appeared in 1992, he wrote that, in order to reflect the changes in relationships and lifestyles that had occurred in the intervening period, the book's title should really be changed to 'Cohabitation, Marriage, Divorce, More Cohabitation, and Probably Remarriage' (1992: vii). As this would obviously have been too long and unwieldy, Cherlin stuck with the original title. But he offers a hypothetical life story to conjure up the increasing diversity of relationships.

> When Bill was ten, his parents separated and divorced. He lived with his mother and saw his father every Saturday. Four years later, his mother remarried, and Bill added a stepfather to his

family. At eighteen, Bill left home to attend college, and after graduation he and his girlfriend moved in together. A year and a half later they married, and soon afterward they had a child. After several years, however, the marriage began to turn sour. Bill and his wife eventually divorced, with Bill's wife retaining custody of the child. Three years later Bill married a woman who had a child from a previous marriage, and together they had another child. Bill's second marriage lasted thirty-five years, until his death.

Cherlin notes that even today such a history is not exactly average or representative of the majority; what is new is that it is not out of the ordinary either.

> Most young people today won't pass through all of the events in this example, but if the levels of marriage, divorce, remarriage, and cohabitation don't decrease in the near future, many will. And many more will have family histories only slightly less complicated. In the 1950s someone with a family history this complex would have been rare; in the 1990s it is no longer unusual. (1992: 4)

If we survey the sociological discussion in the United States, we find that most of Cherlin's colleagues would share his view. But this is not true of family research today in Germany, where polarization and entrenched positions are a common feature and often carry an emotional charge. Debate takes place on such things as values and finer details, but also on the basic framework and the core of research. Many see massive upheavals, perhaps even the end of the traditional family; others, opposing what they call the eternal talk of crisis, maintain that the future belongs with the family; while a third group, lying somewhere in between, prefer to speak of tendencies towards pluralism. What makes this debate especially absorbing is that all sides appeal to empirical data, and in particular to population trends.

I would now first like to consider those interpretations which claim continuity and stability of the family, and to show that they systematically underestimate the elements of change.

17

Then I shall try to develop a perspective that consciously fore-grounds the contemporary dynamic of the family. My aim is not to dramatize the present situation, nor to sound the all-clear, but rather to demonstrate that, although the family lives on, it has become increasingly fragile. In sum, the 'normalization of fragility' is what lies ahead for the family.

Stability of the family – for and against

Arguing over the figures

Those who emphasize stability of the family regard the diag-noses of radical change as little more than a passing fad, an illegitimate extrapolation from individual cases that lacks the solidity of empirical data. In short, the shifts are said to be greatly exaggerated, and the actual trend to be far less spectacu-lar. Here is Norbert F. Schneider:

> This applies, for instance, to the 'ever rising number of divorces', a trend which is more and more often alleged, even though the incidence of divorce in West Germany actually declined be-tween 1984 and 1992. Another example is the repeated claim that the number of 'children of divorced families' is constantly rising. The number has risen, it is true, but an increase from 86,000 in 1970 to 90,000 in 1992 is hardly what I would consider dramatic. (1995: 2)

Now, since the dispute is to a considerable extent about figures, we should begin at the same level and supplement Schneider's figures a little in order to bring out the current and the historical trend. Concerning the children of divorced families, the figure stood at 45,000 in 1960, 92,000 in 1992 and 132,000 in 1998;[1] no great mathematical skills are necessary to see that this has meant a major increase in the space of a few decades. As to the divorce figures, which Schneider considers only up to 1992, we should add that they rose sharply in subsequent years to reach a new historical peak.[2] It is also useful to look at the trend over a longer period.

Table 2.1 Divorces in Germany

Year	Total	Per 10,000 population	Per 10,000 surviving marriages
1900	7,928	1.4	8.1
1920	36,542	5.9	32.1
1930	40,722	6.3	29.5
1950*	84,740	16.9	67.5
1960	48,878	8.8	35.0
1970	76,520	12.6	50.9
1980	96,222	15.6	61.3
1990	125,308	19.4	81.1
1995	147,945	21.9	92.3
1997	161,265	23.7	103.7

* The figures from 1950 refer to West Germany.
Sources: Statistisches Bundesamt (1990: 127); Statistisches Bundesamt (1995b: 108); Emmerling (1999: 39)

The figures in table 2.1 show that the thesis of a major change can claim a solid empirical basis. There is certainly continuity and stability – not of the family, however, but of change itself. Crystallizing more and more clearly in the course of the twentieth century was a rejection of the traditional model of lifelong marriage ('Till death do us part') and a gradual reorientation towards a new model that includes the possibility of divorce (not as an actual aim, only as a tacit option should the need arise); a shift, which Frank F. Furstenberg noted of the USA but which has also become observable in Germany, 'from a bond that lasts a lifetime as a matter of course to one that is maintained only under certain conditions' (1989).

So much for the divorce figures. They can give only a partial picture of the change in lifestyles and relationships, because they show the dissolution only of officially registered and legit-imated marriages. And since the number of non-marital part-nerships has risen sharply in recent years, both in Britain and in Germany,[3] an accurate picture would have to incorporate trends in the break-up of such relationships too.

19

In a family survey conducted by the German Youth Institute, men and women from various age-groups were asked how many partnerships lasting at least one year (whether officially sanctioned or not) they had had in the course of their life so far. The results showed, not altogether surprisingly, that the younger respondents had had a significantly larger number: 'The percentage having had just one relationship declines more or less constantly with each younger age-cohort' (Tölke 1991: 121). But, where there is more experience of relationships, there is also more experience of separation: 'As the beginning of each new relationship is preceded (or for a time accompanied) by the ending of an earlier one, these results mean that young people today have also had much greater experience of separation than in the past' (1991: 123).

A similar tendency is indicated by empirical research of Vaskovics and Rupp (1995) on 'partnership careers', or, to be more precise, on 'the development paths of long-term non-marital relationships'. Although their survey covered only couples with a lifestyle geared to stability,[4] it was found that 'during the four years of observation nearly every fourth couple separated' (1995: 165). Such figures do not, of course, tell us how the people in question experienced the separation – as a liberation or as a misfortune. But they leave no doubt that the number of 'uncertificated marriages' ending in separation is also considerable.

Conceptual elasticity and redefinitions

The sociologist Laszlo Vaskovics is a firm adherent of the 'stability position'. In order to give some idea of this debate beyond the simple dispute over figures, we should look a little more closely at some of his arguments.

In diagnoses stressing radical change in the family, Vascovics sees no more than the long-familiar talk of crises: 'Over the last two centuries, crisis and breakdown of the family have again and again been "detected" and predicted' (1991: 186). He is quite clear about his own conclusions. 'The family as nuclear or conjugal family has kept its dominance up to the present day. … The "normal chaos of love", as it has been called, continues to display clear and dominant patterns of the partnerships which ... in most cases lead to a normal family' (1991: 197).

In order to assess this view of things, it is important to know how Vaskovics defines the 'normal family'. In fact, practically everything goes into his definition. 'With or without a marriage certificate, temporarily or for life, once or a number of times' – everything is indiscriminately included in the nuclear family or its precursors. Even people living alone become 'partnership-oriented' within this framework, because in Vaskovics's view they do not in principle exclude a marital or non-marital relationship and even partly aspire towards one. Most non-marital partnerships are even said to be 'geared to a medium-term perspective'. And, if such couples split up, it can still be assumed 'that they will sooner or later enter into a non-marital long-term relationship with another partner.' Most people living alone have not chosen their situation but have landed in it (usually temporarily) as a result of external events such as divorce or the death of a partner. 'This lifestyle is frequently converted through marriage or remarriage into another family figuration.' As to the decline in birth-rates which has prevailed since the 1960s in Germany and other industrialized countries, the decisive point is that 'parenthood has not ceased to be an important goal for young women and men.' Decisions to postpone the fulfilment of this wish are thus unimportant: 'Why should there be a difference in how late and early parenthood, shorter- and longer-lasting families, are regarded? It is in the nature of things that a family will be started at one point in the life cycle and dissolved at another point.' If ever more men and women remain childless throughout their life, the reason is that childlessness can often be traced to biological problems and is therefore unintended: 'Concealed beneath the fact of childlessness is often an image of the "normal family" that it has not been possible to achieve.' (See Vaskovics 1991: 188–94; 1994: 12.)

Within this conceptual schema, Vaskovics is undoubtedly right that the normal family is alive and flourishing. But the series of redefinitions that allow him to argue this mostly discard what a short time ago constituted the essence of marriage and the family: legal certification, binding force, permanence, and so on. If, amid massive change, all this is simply disregarded, then obviously no change will be left. It will be as in the race between the tortoise and the hare: the normal family is there already. Proof to the contrary is effectively impossible, because everything that looks or could look otherwise is simply built into the original concept.

The result is that the central questions are systematically left out. For example, it is well known from the data available that most men and women do indeed still say that having children is one of their aims in life. The interesting question here is why young people *fail* to achieve this aim more often than previous ones. What are the barriers, the resistances? Or do other goals in life nowadays have greater attraction? Furthermore, it is hardly surprising that most single people do not dismiss all thought of a partnership. But far more intriguing is the question of why they *actually* live alone. What are the resistances or the rival goals? Finally, not much can be said against the statement that every family starts at some point and comes to an end at another. It is as correct as it is trivial. What is not at all trivial is when the family is founded and especially why it is ended – through death or through divorce. How many go on to found another family? How many let it all drop? How many set up several families in succession?

In the account given by Vaskovics, the question in the end is whether the new lifestyles developing today are just the result of external circumstances. Is everything due merely to obstacles in the situation? Are no choices involved? No life projects? And are all those who cannot be fitted into the 'normal family' box simply trying to get into it as quickly as possible? Is everyone's dream to have a nest like that of their parents and grandparents? And will those whose dreams are today slightly different sooner or later find themselves back with the old ones?

If such questions are not asked, if instead all forms of private life (with or without a partner, with or without a certificate, with or without permanence) are bunched together under the heading of the 'normal family', then all contours go by the board. Change? The perspective does not allow for it. And so it comes nowhere into view.

The dynamic of family development

It may be thought that, since the data themselves are not in dispute, the argument over figures, comparisons and concepts is in itself rather pointless, a version of the well-known question whether the glass is half full or half empty. But it can also be seen in a different and more productive light – that is, as implicitly or explicitly concerned with the direction of development or the underlying dynamic. What is at issue are not only well-known figures but data that no one yet knows about the future of the family and people's lifestyles; not only the current state of the glass but the state that can be expected to develop. In short, is the glass being filled or emptied? Which tendency is operating in the given situation?

We shall now look at this question in greater detail as it involves relationships between couples. Should we expect a strengthening and stabilization of such relationships, or on the contrary growing discontinuity, change and fragility? Which tendency is discernible today?

The normalization of divorce

If we take historical trends since the nineteenth century, it is not hard to see that, in Britain as in other Western countries, a massive change has taken place in the institutional bases of marriage. Whereas in the nineteenth century strong normative regulations – especially church influences and legal provisions – preserved marriage at least as an external scaffolding (one might perhaps say a straitjacket), this whole structure gradually crumbled in the course of the twentieth century. In other words, taboos and barriers which used to make divorce more difficult, or often altogether impossible, have been progressively dismantled (Blasius 1992; Coester-Waltjen 1994).

There is much evidence to suggest that this process has been driven not least by a number of interacting seesaw effects. Simplifying a great deal, we may say that social conditions associated with modernity (industrialization, urbanization,

23

secularization, etc.) gradually produced a need among individuals for divorce; that is, an initially tiny but slowly rising number of men and women were no longer willing to preserve marriage under all circumstances but were prepared to seek a divorce. This set up a pressure on the institutions of society (state, politics, law) to modify the highly restrictive legislation governing marriage, the family and divorce. To be sure, this trend did not assert itself in a unilinear way and initially ran up against strong opposition. But, as the law finally changed, a new period began in which different norms and moral conceptions were codified, the opposition to divorce lost much of its power to influence behaviour, and a tacit normalization of divorce gradually came about. In a further stage, growing demand for divorce again put pressure on the legal system to abolish institutional hurdles and to fall more into line with people's wishes.

Gertrud Nunner-Winkler is one of those who have analysed such processes of interaction (1989). She argues that, once divorce becomes easier to obtain, an upward pressure is created which is almost self-reinforcing, as the area of free choice is opened wider and wider. This means that the new possibilities for separation and divorce have an effect beneath the surface even when they are initially taken up only to a very limited extent. Their mere visibility (powerfully enhanced by the modern mass media) ensures that traditional lifestyles and marriages are not left unaffected. Anyone today who keeps up a marriage does so in the knowledge that there are ways out of it, that there are other ways of acting. Thus, since the continuation of a marriage expresses a conscious choice, it too comes under pressure to justify itself.

This increased requirement for justification drives the spiral of change ever onward. To maintain a tradition, it is enough that nothing should go badly wrong; to justify elective behaviour, positive reasons are needed. Or, in this connection, a pre-established marital situation is accepted so long as it is not unbearable, whereas a freely chosen one must prove itself to be the best on the horizon of alternative possibilities. The simple compulsion to justify thus pushes further upward the yardstick by which happiness is measured, with the result that more marriages appear inadequate and people become more willing to contemplate divorce. 'New norms arise which make divorce acceptable or even essential under certain circumstances' (Furstenberg 1989).

Effects of mutual reinforcement or amplification have also been identified by Diekmann and Engelhardt in their use of German Youth Institute data to analyse divorce risks. The empirical material, they claim, points to a kind of 'divorce spiral', an 'independent dynamic' or 'self-supporting process unleashed by social-demographic change' (1995a: 215). Once a certain threshold is crossed, a series of snowball effects continually augment the risks of divorce. Thus, in societies where divorce is a rare exception, divorced people have to face a loss of standing and reputation as they find themselves socially declassed; but, as the frequency of divorce increases, such stigmatization tends to subside (not all at once, but gradually over the decades). From being a drastic transgression, divorce becomes one possible component of a bourgeois existence. This change in the social climate then also makes divorce easier for those who would otherwise never have dared to take the step – hence the snowball effect whereby the fewer the penalties to be expected from divorce, the more frequent it becomes. The same applies to the chances of finding a new partner, for the search becomes easier as the rising divorce figures remove the stigma and increase the number of men and women free of marital ties. But, if divorce no longer leads more or less inevitably to a single existence but holds out the chance of remarriage, then the costs associated with it diminish – which in turn raises further the number of those willing to extricate themselves from an unsatisfactory marriage (1995a: 216).

Self-protective strategies

When divorce becomes more common and can be directly observed in one's own personal milieu (a school friend or sister or perhaps even one's own parents), when the media openly discuss divorce and the tabloids make a mint out of the marital dramas of public figures (from Prince Charles to Liz Taylor), it becomes evident even in the smallest village that marriage is no longer necessarily for life. Moreover, this dawning awareness is not likely to remain without direct effects. Gradually, to some extent covertly, people begin to adjust their behaviour to the risk of divorce. They want to make provisions in advance. And, since divorce is not something that anyone consciously hopes for, they try to protect themselves against it.

According to Jürgen Schumacher, couples increasingly develop strategies to 'minimize the risks associated with relationships, which have become higher than ever before' (1981: 503). This does not mean that they are less willing to enter into a relationship, but rather that they avoid as much as possible the creation of barriers that 'excessively increase ... the costs of readjustment' in the event of separation (509). Therefore relationships and lifestyles are chosen which allow for separation in case of need – or, to put it more bluntly, which factor in the possibility of separation. Since two events – formal marriage and the birth of children – raise special obstacles to separation, it is easy to see why more and more couples are staying away from the registry office and postponing or renouncing any idea of having children. The declining inclination both to marry and to bear children, which can be seen from demographic data, may in this sense be interpreted as a risk-diminishing strategy. To take precautions today, in the face of the fragility of relationships, means to avoid obstacles that might 'limit the room for manoeuvre in future adjustment decisions' (509). To live in a relationship while keeping the exit door open: this is becoming the new motto, even if it is not so often spoken aloud.

Diekmann and Engelhardt also examine these kinds of protective strategy, but go one stage further to consider their likely consequences. Again they identify a snowball effect that pushes the divorce figures still higher. 'If a married couple have doubts about the durability of their relationship, these will crystallize in a narrowing of "marital investments". But this itself increases the actual risk of divorce' (1995a: 216). Freely translated, this means: the greater the doubt, the higher the eventual instability. The less that is put into life together (through children, home ownership, etc.), the less there is to keep the couple together.[5] With less to lose, it is easier to separate.

Diekmann and Engelhardt see a similar interaction between female employment and the risk of divorce: 'It can be empirically shown that the "anticipation" of divorce risks encourages the tendency of married women to undertake paid employment – a fact which in turn presumably increases the risk of divorce' (1995a: 216). Or, to put it in another way, the evolution of divorce-rates translates into a learning effect for the planning of young women's lives. The more fragile the role of the family is felt to be, the less prepared young women are to rely entirely upon marriage and the stronger is their orientation to other perspectives in life such as a career of their own. The result is that, in the event of an outbreak of conflict, the woman is no longer unconditionally tied to the marriage but can also choose to end it.

In their statistical analysis, Diekmann and Engelhardt further establish that cohabitation before marriage considerably increases the likelihood of divorce: 'It is striking that married persons who lived together before marriage present a 40–60 per cent higher risk of divorce' (1995b: 4). The authors themselves, not expecting this result, had assumed that a period of living together before marriage would tell a couple whether or not they were suited to each other. But, if we consider the individualist ethic that underlies both choices of action, it becomes quite clear why the risk of divorce rises with a trial marriage.[6] Anyone who does not see marriage beforehand as a sacrament, as a sacred or at least quite special kind of bond, is more prepared to live with someone without an official certificate; and, should the couple later marry, they will not suddenly begin to see marriage as a sacrament but will be more prepared to contemplate divorce if the worst comes to the worst. Conversely, anyone who believes that marriage should be based on feelings and personal harmony will think it sensible to test out the feelings in everyday life before entering into an official contract; and will also tend to think that the marriage has become empty and pointless if, under certain circumstances (routinization, money shortage, irritating children), the feelings change and the passion departs.

27

We may conclude, then, that risk-reducing strategies have the paradoxical effect of making divorce more likely. Does this mean that men and women become entangled in their own strategies and traps? Does the very behaviour that is supposed to limit risk end up multiplying it? Yes and no. For, although it increases the chance of eventual separation, it also keeps its resulting costs lower. People who do not formally marry will never be put through all the legal procedures of divorce or the financial burdens (court costs, solicitors' fees, etc.). People who have no children will never have to negotiate custody, endure separation or struggle through as a single parent. Women who go out to work during marriage will not, in the event of divorce, have to search around on the job market or sue for maintenance from a former partner.

As these examples show, the risk-reducing strategies prompted by the higher incidence of divorce have a dual effect. On the one hand, they contribute to the higher incidence of divorce and endanger the couple's relationship in the long term. But if we take separately the two individuals affected we see at once that they are better prepared for the eventuality of divorce, better forearmed for living alone again. In this sense, the risk-reducing strategies both generate and diminish the risks. They may better be seen as protective strategies, with an individualist logic at their core. What they promote is not the couple's stability but the individuality of each part of the couple, in the face of the unpredictable turns and accidents of the relationship.

The generation effect

Empirical studies have clearly demonstrated that a kind of 'social heredity' affects the risk of divorce. Men and women who have experienced a divorce in their own original family are themselves much more likely to divorce in later life than are men and women whose parents stayed together. A number of (not mutually exclusive) approaches may be used to account for this phenomenon (e.g. Diekmann and Engelhardt 1995a; Fthenakis 1995). Here we shall mainly stick to the socialization hypothesis, which starts from experiences in childhood and youth and stresses a learning model for behaviour with regard to marriage, family and relationships.

Of relevance is family therapy material which shows that, among children from broken homes, 'there is a lasting disturbance to their trust in relationships and the possibility of constructively solving conflicts.' For example, they often have a hidden dread of separation and handle it 'by clinging more strongly to their partner, who often feels obliged to withdraw and thus (paradoxically) to confirm the fears.' This kind of vicious circle is indeed a traditional symptom among divorced families (Reich 1991: 83). But, in relation to the psychological study of relationships, one might perhaps also interpret it in another way (see e.g. Stierlin 1995). Because children with divorced parents develop less security in relationships than other children, they tend to deal with relationships in an unstable way, swinging from one extreme to the other, and this results in disappointments.

A large-scale survey of what girls and women plan for their lives came up with some interesting results (Seidenspinner and Burger 1982: report, 60ff). Comparing girls from intact families with daughters of single mothers, the study showed that the latter placed greater value on autonomy and had greater reservations about marriage and motherhood. 'They can obviously imagine other things in life for themselves than marriage, and their marked striving for professional and financial independence fit in very well with this.... They want to rely on their own efforts and achievements.... Many of them, with their mother's life in mind, consciously do not want to marry. Their wish to have children [is] markedly weaker than among other girls.' Here there has clearly been a learning effect, which means that relationships take second place to a life of their own. Self-protective strategies have priority – which, as we have seen, increases the risk of divorce in the event of marriage.

The rising number of divorces has led in recent studies to a greater focus on the long-term consequences for children, on the psychological and emotional traces left behind. So far no single answer has emerged from such studies; in fact, the various authors come up with quite different results. Many conclude that, when marriages break down early on, the children tend to be sensitive and vulnerable, often remaining disturbed for the rest of their lives (e.g. Wallerstein and Blakeslee 1989; Napp-Peters 1995). Others suggest that the children are likely to turn out more robust and capable of adjustment; that, although the post-divorce period is one of dramatic crises, they usually get over it and settle down in the new conditions (e.g. Furstenberg and Cherlin 1991).

Here I would like to propose a third interpretation which, in keeping with the points made so far, takes social heredity as central to the risk of divorce. Early experiences of separation involve socialization of a particular kind, at the core of which stands the individualist message. Thus, if children manage to come to terms with changing family forms, they will learn – involuntarily and painfully, to be sure – how to end relationships and cope with loss. They will learn at an early age what desertion and parting mean, and consider it a fact of life that love does not last for ever, that relationships come to an end, that separation is a normal event. They will be used to living with change and not 'taking it tragically'. They will be able to say of their own family history: 'My first father, my real one, left my mother. Later my mother told my stepfather to leave. And now things are shaky again between my mother and the man who's living with us for the moment. You get used to stuff like that.'[7] As one generation succeeds the next, children become experts in change. And, in so far as they mentally prepare themselves to keep pain at bay, they develop their own kinds of self-assertion and self-defence.

Socialization effects of this kind may be seen in various lights. According to the positive interpretation, children from families whose parents have separated – especially the daughters – learn that a full and satisfying life is also possible alone, without a partner, and that they do not necessarily have to depend on the success of a long-term relationship. They learn to prepare themselves for an independent life, instead of seeing their identity only in the family. According to the negative interpretation, such children lack security in relationships, social skills and the ability to deal with conflict; instead of finding new models for themselves, they basically repeat the mistakes of their parents. Now, the two interpretations do not necessarily exclude each other: it may be the case that daughters of single mothers gain greater independence but less ability to handle conflict. But, whichever interpretation or combination of the two one chooses, they all point to the same conclusion: namely, that divorce fosters the learning of individualist attitudes, which in the next generation leads to further divorces. Or, more generally, however great may be the differences between the various explanatory approaches to divorce risk and social heredity, they are in striking agreement that 'the research results suggest a dynamic that will further weaken the established family structures' (Fthenakis 1995: 143).

The complex relations of a divorced family

Upheaval and a new beginning

When a divorce occurs, the situations of men and women, parents and children develop in different directions. First of all, in a directly geographical sense, one partner (nearly always the man) moves to another dwelling and perhaps another town (in order to make a fresh start). Women and children remain behind, but it is not uncommon for them too to move at a later date (to somewhere cheaper, or closer to the grandparents, and so on) – which therefore means a change in surroundings, school and neighbours. Moreover, the new economic circumstances usually bring a fall in income, the extent of which varies according to the laws in force in the particular country. In the United States, the standard of living sharply declines for women and children, while it not infrequently rises for men (because often they pay no maintenance) (Cherlin 1992: 73–4). In Britain, where the Child Support Agency has responsibility for collecting payments from non-resident parents (usually fathers), numerous weaknesses in the agency's performance have caused hardship to many families, and most people are financially worse off after divorce. In Germany too there is something like a distribution of hardship, with men also usually having to take a financial loss, but still women and children mostly fare markedly worse (Lucke 1990).

In addition, a new organization of everyday life becomes necessary after a divorce. This must be negotiated, and not infrequently fought over, between the two who used to be a couple. Who gets the house or flat, what part of the household goods, what keepsakes? How much maintenance must be paid to whom? Above all, who gets the children and how will custody rights be defined? Man against woman. Claims and counter-claims are asserted, rights and duties distributed. New agreements are sought, and often also disputed. Instead of a common daily life and a common abode together, there are separate visiting times for the father. When may he come, and for how long? How much time should the child spend with him at weekends and holidays? In extreme cases, the man or woman even tries to settle things by force; the number of parental kidnappings is also on the increase.

Family therapists, lawyers and judges see every day how feelings of hurt and bitterness, rage and hate can escalate between ex-partners after a divorce. But, even when the separation takes place in a calm and rational way, the act of divorce inevitably constitutes a new relationship between the man, woman and children. Much more plainly than before, they confront one another as individuals eager to assert their own interests and pursuits, their own wishes and rights. The former partners have not only different ideas about the future but also different images of their time together in the past, and often different allocations of blame and general perceptions of each other (he always fooled around with other women, she always threw money down the drain).

In between stand the children, also with their own wishes. As a number of studies have shown, they usually hope that their parents will make it up. But it is a vain hope: the parents go their own way, and the children must learn to live with divided loyalties. When fights break out over who they should stay with, they are often asked in court whether they would prefer to be with their mother or their father. However carefully it is done, they are expected to make some statement against the one or the other – and, in less considerate cases, they feel the parents' manoeuvres and direct attempts to sway them. When visiting rules are established but the ex-partners are unable to get over their hurt, the children are drawn into the post-divorce battlefield, sounded out about the lifestyle and new liaisons of the former spouse, bribed with special treats, used as bearers of information between the warring fronts. Nor is that always all. In some families, the children are divided up between the former partners, so that even siblings may find themselves separated from each other. But far more often the relationship with the father rapidly tails off after the divorce; he simply disappears from the children's field of vision. The link to the paternal grandparents also grows weaker and more problematic, in part consciously undermined by the mother to wipe out all reference to the father.[8]

All this together means that one thing is certain after divorce: namely, that everything will become uncertain and fluid; nothing will be the same as before.

Conjugal succession and elective affinities

Many divorced people later remarry or cohabit with a new partner who was also married before and who brings other children into the relationship. More and more children thus grow up with one non-biological parent. According to recent findings, such stepfamilies are 'a curious example of an organizational merger; they join family cultures into a single household' (Furstenberg and Cherlin 1991: 83). Here too, differing values, rules and routines, expectations and everyday practices – from table manners and pocket money to television viewing and bedtime hours – have to be negotiated and agreed. This, to be sure, is far from being always easy – on the contrary: 'the likelihood of clashes in habits and outlook is considerable' (Giddens 1997: 157). There are also rules about how the various parties should interact with each other – partners with ex-partners, partners of ex-partners with each other, children from the different relationships with each other, especially in the case of stepchildren. Again and again, questions arise that touch people's sore spots and demand delicate balancing acts: 'Should a child call a new step-parent by name, or is "Dad" or "Mum" more appropriate? Should the step-parent discipline the children as a natural parent would? How should a step-parent treat the new spouse of his or her previous partner when collecting the children?' (1997: 157).

In addition, many children move backwards and forwards between their different family worlds, between the 'everyday parent' who has custody and lives with a new partner, and the 'weekend parent' who does not have custody and may also have a new family. This may well lead to complex relationship structures presentable only in the form of a diagram with many ramifications. 'Marriage and divorce chains', 'conjugal succession', 'multiparent families', 'patchwork families' – all these are concepts designed to make the new family forms easier to grasp. One key feature, of course, is that it is not clear who actually belongs to the family. There is no longer one single definition – that has been lost somewhere in the rhythm of separations and new relationships. Instead, each member has their own definition of who belongs to the family; everyone lives out their own version of the patch-work family.

> Let us consider the case in which a married couple with two children divorces and the wife retains custody of the children. … If we ask the divorced mother who is in her immediate family, she certainly would include her children, but she might well exclude her ex-husband, who now lives elsewhere. If we ask her children who is in their immediate family, however, we might get a different answer. If the children still see their father regularly, they probably would include both their father and their mother as part of their family. And if we ask the ex-husband who is in his immediate family, he might include his children, whom he continues to see, but not his ex-wife. Thus, after divorce, mother, father, and children each may have a

different conception of who is in their immediate family. In fact, one can no longer define 'the family' or 'the immediate family' except in relation to a particular person. (Cherlin 1992: 73–4)

What we see here, then, is how 'the' idea of the family breaks up into separate pieces and varying perspectives.

A woman who originally comes from a post-divorce family and herself now lives in one has depicted this situation in the diagram on p. 36.

In this constellation it is no longer the traditional rules of ascription (parentage and marriage) which determine kinship. The key factor now is whether the social relations stemming from it persist after the divorce. Where these relations are broken or gradually fade, there is also an end to the ties of kinship. What could be seen emerging in other family constellations of modernity is here fully displayed: maintenance of the family tie is no longer a matter of course but a freely chosen act. In the situation following a divorce, kinship is worked out anew in accordance with the laws of choice and personal inclination – it takes the form of 'elective affinities'. As it is no longer given as a destiny, it requires a greater personal contribution, more active care. As one study of patchwork families puts it: 'From the huge universe of potential kin, people actively create kin by establishing a relationship – by working at becoming kin. And they have wide latitude in choosing which links to activate' (Furstenberg and Cherlin 1991: 93). Many relatives by the first marriage continue to be 'part of the family'; many by the second marriage are added to them; and others remain outside or drop out.

The upshot is no longer determined in advance. For, where there is a choice, personal preferences more and more become the yardstick; each individual draws his or her own boundaries. Even children growing up in the same household no longer necessarily have the same definition of who is one of the family (Furstenberg and Cherlin 1991: 93). What all this means is that 'conjugal succession implies greater fluidity and uncertainty in kinship relations. Cultivating family ties may become more important as less can be taken for

Me

Me, my brother,
my mother, her husband
and our half-sister

Me, my husband,
his son and our son

Me, my brother, my father,
his wife, our two half-brothers
and our half-sister

Figure 2.1   My family
Source: Reberg (1997: 118)

granted about the obligation of particular kin to one another' (Furstenberg 1989: 28–9). This confronts everyone involved with new questions and brings new decision-making processes into play.

Management of feelings and relationships

Even if the so-called normal family is not a locus of constant affection, it is generally clear that all the individuals in question belong to it and are responsible for one another, and that their feelings at least should be of a certain kind.

This is not how things are in the succession family. Here the relations are much more complicated, above all because divorce dissolves the bond between adults but not between parents and children. When new partners and children then come along – mother's boyfriend and father's woman, my, your, our children – a new network of competing responsibilities, feelings and loyalties comes into being. If resources are tight, as they nearly always are, a choice then has to be made between previous family ties and new ones. Presents, holiday visits, financial support, time: whose claims should take precedence, whose should be seen as less important? As nothing binding settles this in advance, people have to experiment and work it out for themselves. New rules of solidarity and loyalty become necessary. As one study puts it:

> It will be extraordinarily interesting to see the relative strength of consanguinal and affinal bonds within families whose members have been multiplied by successive marriages. How will grandparents divide their inheritance among biological grandchildren whom they barely know, stepgrandchildren acquired early in life, or stepgrandchildren acquired from their own second marriage who have helped to nurse them later in life? Do biological fathers have more obligation to send their biological children, who have been raised by a stepfather, to college or their own stepchildren whom they have raised? (Furstenberg 1989: 28–9)

What seems so matter-of-fact on paper is probably the cause of much turmoil in reality, especially as it concerns not only the allocation of goods but also that which they in part symbolize, rightly or wrongly, for the individuals at issue: namely, the continuation or withdrawal of care and affection (why didn't Dad write to me on my birthday, even if he's living somewhere else?).[9] Since the divorce has taught the children that a sudden reversal of feelings is possible, they have become basically insecure and prone to doubt and feelings of hurt, disappointment, jealousy and rage. Often the parents prefer not to know about all that, for it reminds them of their own guilty conscience, their own sense of hurt. So the children too have to start allocating feelings in carefully measured doses, expressing or concealing them according to the situation. They must learn that they cannot communicate a lot of what is agitating them – perhaps even the thing that agitates them most of all. As they move between different, often mutually hostile sides, they must learn to be cautious and dexterous, to find the right direction among contradictory signals. You shouldn't trust Daddy, says the mother. I can't tell Mum that, because it'll make her cry. I also want to say 'Daddy' to Paul, Mummy's new man – but what if my real father gets to hear of it?

The rules cannot be looked up in some book. And whereas children can get help from their parents on other matters – not always, but at least some of the time – the parents are far too emotionally involved to give them advice on these more delicate issues. It may be possible to swap experiences with a brother or sister who is around, or perhaps with other children of the same age who are in a similar family situation. But whether the youngsters excel in the management of feelings and relationships in the complicated network of conjugal succession, or whether they remain awkward and insecure, they have to fend for themselves much of the time in the competition between divided loyalties. They may feel abandoned or they may become more independent in the process – or perhaps both together. In any event, they no longer experience the old family model as something to be taken for granted. As one generation succeeds the next, it is again an individualist message that is conveyed.

From the normal biography to the do-it-yourself biography

If the above account is accepted, it follows that a special kind of dynamic is involved in current family trends. The fragility of the traditional model of the family will become more pronounced, further breaks will occur and affect groups that have hitherto remained stable. Lives such as those described by Andrew Cherlin in the story quoted at the beginning do not constitute some kind of American exceptionalism. Perhaps they will not be as common in Europe as they are in the USA, but here too they will become more common. Succession families, multi-parent families, patchwork families will also spread here, together with the complex genealogies and colourful networks associated with them.

This does not exclude, indeed makes more likely, the appearance of counter-trends and the development of hopes and longings that the family will be a haven in the stormy seas of the modern world, a source of re-enchantment in a world that has lost its magic. Here no more than anywhere else, however, is a wish the same as its fulfilment. And it must remain doubtful whether such attempts at counter-modernization will be successful, whether a revival of the traditional family model will occur among whole sections of the population and not just in isolated cases. For the very yearnings in question do not emerge in a social vacuum outside politics, the media, the legal system, and so on, but are entangled in the same set of social conditions which have produced the cracks in the traditional model of the family. Flights from modernity are themselves part of modernity – and therefore involve contradictions of a special kind.

The diagnosis presented here for the area of couples, marriage and the family – more instability, more change, more transitions and intermediate forms in the course of people's lives – is in essence strikingly similar to that which has been put forward for other areas of modern society. Take, for example, the findings of recent research on work. Whereas in the post-war period a stable working life was the rule, the period since the late 1970s has seen a growing erosion of the 'normal work situation' (that is, long-term full-time employment protected by social and labour legislation). By virtue of deregulation and flexibilization in the labour market, more varied and unstable forms of employment have come to the fore. These can no longer be understood within the old categories – here work, there unemployment – and involve what has been called 'a new topography of work'. 'A variety of "precarious", "atypical", "non-standard" work situations have increasingly established themselves between the normal work situation of old and statistically recorded official unemployment' (Osterland 1991: 353). Similarly, recent research on poverty has shown that in our society it often lasts not for a lifetime but for limited periods of time, and therefore threatens wider sections of the population through a kind of 'democratization of poverty'. 'Situations of poverty are probably more "mobile" than it has hitherto been assumed. Poverty is often only an episode in a person's life.... As a temporary state and a latent risk, poverty reaches into middle layers of society and is no longer confined to traditional marginal groups or an excluded bottom third' (Leibfried et al. 1995: 9). Seen in this way, poverty is becoming time-specific, less a permanent fate than a phase in life. 'Situations of poverty thus prove to be a complex web consisting of phases of actual poverty, interruptions, relapses and sometimes final exits' (1995: 81)

The parallel is obvious enough. What is said here about poverty could apply in almost the same words to the family. Indeed, one of the conclusions of recent research is that the family is becoming a 'transitional phase in life' (Nave-Herz 1992: 190) or a 'part-time community' (Imhof 1988: 57). The traditional family, it is suggested, will not disappear but become less common, because other lifestyles and types of relationship are developing alongside it. It will tie many people not for their whole lives but only during certain periods and phases.

In the end, these various facets add up to a coherent picture. The general diagnosis is that people's lives are becoming more mobile, more porous, and of course more fragile. In the place of pre-given and often compulsory types of relationship is appearing the 'until the next thing' principle, as Bauman calls it, a kind of refusal of lifelong plans, permanent ties, immutable identities.[10] When divorce becomes normal and what used to be called normal starts to crumble at more and more levels, then 'life is a building-site'.[11] Instead of fixed forms, more individual choices, more beginnings and more farewells. Above all, more soaring flights and crashing falls, more search operations. From the normal biography to the 'do-it-yourself' biography: this is the hallmark of modernity.[12] Perhaps it is also its identity-producing core, beyond all episodes, stages and breaks.

3

Life as a Planning Project

If it is true, as we have argued, that the barriers on the road to modernity which used to be set by nature, religion or tradition have been losing more and more of their power and strength; if new options and individual choices are appearing in their place; if personal lifestyles, and not least relationships, thereby become more open and mobile as well as more fragile; if they can now in principle be terminated and are always beset with the risk of loss and breakdown – what does this mean for the ways in which people conduct themselves in everyday life? How do men and women deal with the 'risky freedoms' that have come about through the processes of individualization? How do they react to the 'manufactured insecurity' (Beck 1994; Giddens 1994b) that marks the age of advanced modernity?

The first answer is that individualization produces a striving for security, which may take a number of forms. First of all, the need for security is translated into demands on the state or various public institutions, in the expectation that they should protect the individual through a network of services and provisions, rules and regulations (Zapf 1994; Hesse 1994). Since the state cannot, however, hold off all risks, dangers, questions and doubts, since some insecurity always remains, many take flight into fundamentalist ideologies or esoteric movements and seek reassurance in magic, myth or metaphysics. But apart from such attempts to abolish insecurity altogether, modernity has also created its own model of behaviour for actively coping with the uncertainties of life under conditions of individualization. Its watchwords are: Plan! Bring the future under control! Protect yourself from accidents – steer and direct them!

In short, life is supposed to become a planning project. This chapter will look at what such planning involves, how it expresses itself, and especially what it means in the realm of personal relations between men and women, parents and children.

The rise of the idea of planning

Since 'life as a planning project' has its social roots in the individualization drive of modernity, it is important to begin by defining more clearly what is meant by individualization. A brief summary for our present purposes[1] would be that individualization expands the radius of people's lives, their leeway for action and choice, but certainly does not mean 'a logic of unrestricted juggling in almost free space',[2] a limitless acting out of personal desires, nor mere 'subjectivity' as if there were not 'beneath the surface of lifeworlds a highly efficient, closely meshed institutional society'.[3] In fact, the space in which modern subjects move with their options for action is anything but a space outside society. The density of regulations in modern society is well known and even notorious (from the MOT through tax returns to rubbish-sorting requirements), the total effect being an extremely complex artifact with labyrinthine structures, which literally accompanies us from cradle to grave (no existence without certificates of birth and death). And on top of the official regulations are the more subtle norms constructed by mass media, advertising and consumption.

Active handling of institutional guidelines

If individual lives, both now and previously, have been subject to various social guidelines, what is so special about contemporary life under conditions of individualization? First of all, the guidelines are no longer set by class, religion and tradition, but rather by the labour market, the welfare state, the educational system, the judicial system, and so on. Second, the crucial feature of these modern guidelines is that individuals must to some extent produce them through action of their own and incorporate them into their own life history. The traditional guidelines of pre-industrial society often involved rigorous limits or even barriers to action, such as the marriage prohibitions that applied to wide sections of the population, or the sartorial regulations that in some countries prescribed in detail what the lower classes were permitted to wear. By contrast, the institutional guidelines of modern society are more in the way of services or inducements to action: one thinks, for example, of the welfare state, unemployment benefit, education grants or savings incentives. To put it simply, whereas people used to be *born* into a number of social givens (such as class or religion), they now have to *do* something, to make an effort of their own – for example, by maintaining their position on the labour market, or by applying for housing benefit and giving reasons why they should receive it. Here it is necessary to know how to assert oneself, to prevail in the competition for scarce resources. Or, in Parsonian terms, it is now mainly a question of acquired rather than ascribed positions.

Anyone unable to make this kind of acquisition, however, finds their position under threat. Anyone unable to keep up with the institutional guidelines of modern society – that is, not sufficiently flexible to handle them properly – has to suffer the consequences in their personal life. They risk losing their job, income and social position. As Ulrich Beck puts it: individuals 'must learn, on pain of permanent disadvantage, to think of themselves as action centres, as planning offices in relation to their own lives, their own capacities, orientations, relationships, and so on' (1986a: 217). When a person's life is no longer so much a destiny as an area of possibility, this calls for new skills and new ways of behaving and thinking. In the expanded field of options, individuals have increasingly to work through their own courses of action, and to perform varied feats of coordination and integration. More and more, the advance of modernity requires an active, self-driven conduct of life which skilfully takes up and deploys, and if necessary also fends off, the institutional givens. Martin Kohli has expressed this in a succinct formula: 'Life is no longer … "a wonderful gift from God" but an individual possession that has to be constantly defended. More, the shaping of life becomes an individual task and project' (1986: 185).

Forced into the future

In this sense, individualization also crucially involves a breaking away from earlier forms of communally organized life and provision – from the family as a work-based or economic community, supported in emergencies by the village or kin (Borscheid 1988). When these reference points start to crumble, the securing of existence becomes mainly the task of individuals, who have to assert themselves and rely on their own achievements to earn a livelihood. In the first phase of industrialized societies, this applies mainly to the family's male 'breadwinner', in accordance with the model of bourgeois society. But today women too, in however contradictory ways, are permitted or required to make a living for themselves. Only in the event of real collapse is the individual entitled to call upon the assistance of the state (and, as this is fenced in with conditions, restrictions and interpretations, it is by no means always claimed).

This being so, individuals have an interest in developing strategies to 'cover' themselves and their possessions (as Kohli puts it), to preserve the means of their long-term livelihood. As this makes it important to have protection against potential risks and dangers, a major part of any such strategy is thought about the future, a kind of early warning system that can enable risks to be dealt with and rendered harmless. Not by chance has 'prevention', understood as a combination of foresight and forearming, become such a fashionable keyword in the individualized society. Calculation and control: this planning dimension is forcing individuals into the future as they go about their everyday lives.

Berger, Berger and Kellner write (1975: 66): 'In modern society the planning of life has become a value in itself.... A remarkably large percentage of discussions among members of a family ... refer to future perspectives in life. The life-plan is being continually revised.' But there is also a reverse side: 'Lack of such a life-plan is generally a reason for disapproval.' Someone who fails to plan is increasingly suspect in the modern way of thinking and is usually labelled 'naïve', 'irrational' or even 'irresponsible'. In case of doubt, he or she has to bear the consequences – no longer a victim of fate, but 'personally to blame'.

The spread of expert knowledge

In the disenchanted world of modernity, one is supposed to plan, to look ahead, to act with a goal in mind. But how is this possible? The answer, at least at first sight, is that secularization processes have made the guiding agents in society themselves secular; they are now called specialists, experts or advisers, and their rise is one of the striking features of the times. They reach into literally all of life's niches and pursuits, from fashion and clothing to consumption, leisure and travel, from diet and upbringing to sport and gymnastics, and then right into the most intimate areas of love, sexuality and relationships. This omnipresence of advisers is not difficult to understand, for anyone who has to plan must first gather information, weigh, filter and compare it, and if necessary gather some more.

Our world today, writes Anthony Giddens, is 'a world of clever people'. He explains that he does not mean people are more intelligent than they used to be, but that with detraditionalization and individualization expert knowledge has become more and more a part of everyday life. 'Expertise does not remain the sole province of the expert; ... every lay individual can also, in principle and often in practice, appropriate expert knowledge to be applied in the context of social activities' (1994a: 95).

Experts offer promises for a healthy diet and bargain shopping, for success at work and correct childrearing, for a slim

46

figure, happy relationships and ways of handling psychological crises. They throw up theories, strategies and solutions; enumerate advantages and disadvantages; provide recipes and rules; show ways forward and ways out. In short, they offer practical help on how to make the best of life and to perform the necessary calculations.

But is that what experts actually help people to do? That is the question – and a sweeping answer would certainly be inappropriate. At least it is clear that the knowledge they offer is fundamentally different from the traditional guidelines that used to be given. For however much security it promises, however many certificates and seals of approval it can invoke, such knowledge is by its very nature always uncertain. There are two reasons for this (Giddens 1994a: 95). First, expert knowledge is not static but expanding – which means that it may also age and become outdated. To take one especially striking case, a few decades ago some doctors were still advising patients to smoke for physical and mental relaxation (Giddens 1994b: 88), but today sombre warnings are attached to all tobacco advertising: 'Tobacco seriously damages health.' Similarly, with breast-feeding, mothers were first told to keep to a strict regime with fixed hours, but now this is regarded as damaging to the baby's progress and breast-feeding on demand is the motto. The examples could be multiplied almost endlessly. Nor is it only along the temporal axis that we find a reversal of rules and recommendations; even at the same point in time we are faced with the conflicting views of rival experts, who all promise certain knowledge but in reality, when one compares the information, often present more contradictions than knowledge. What is then left behind are irritation, confusion, doubt: 'There are no experts of all experts to show us the way' (Giddens 1994a: 96). As this is inevitably the case, expert knowledge can never attain the degree of certainty and legitimacy that the old guidelines used to have. Furthermore, expert knowledge is becoming ever narrower, ever more specialized, and this increases the risk of unintended consequences. Expertise 'is increasingly more focused, and is liable to produce unintended and unforeseen outcomes which cannot be contained – save for the development of further expertise, thereby repeating the same phenomenon' (Giddens 1991: 31).

Expert knowledge is thus always, if one may say so, in the process of breaking up. Normally this may remain concealed for a long time, but then a sudden crisis will make it evident as the experts publicly air their disputes. This hardly needs to be emphasized after Chernobyl, AIDS and BSE. How harmful are certain toxins? What are the routes of infection? Who is most at risk? How can people protect themselves? The experts can go on fighting it out, but ordinary people have to choose how to behave (in matters of sexuality, diet or childrearing, for example), how to shape their lives. They are called upon to be 'responsible citizens', well informed and rationally deliberative, but what information can they trust? There are more and more situations where the responsible citizen (not least the caring mother) feels lost in a jungle of expert advice yet is compelled to choose only one path – either alone or through discussing with other individuals or self-help groups; perhaps boldly and self-confidently, perhaps feeling insecure and bewildered.

One way or another, however, the social landscape is changing for ever. Since expert opinions – unlike church dogma, for example – do not proclaim the one and only truth but offer rival definitions and statements, the stability of the old univocal framework is falling apart. Responsible citizens behave some in this way, some in another, and always with good reasons for what they decide. The leeway for individual action is thus expanding as ever more paths open up, intersect, run in parallel and then move apart. A new confusion grows up together with the new uncertainty.

Precautions in personal relationships

Let us now consider how ways of planning the future work out in people's personal lives, and what new patterns of behaviour can be discerned in this field. The key question is how the fact of being 'forced into the future', this normative requirement of modern life, expresses itself in everyday behaviour. What strategies, and perhaps also dilemmas, are displayed in it?

Testing relationships

Let us begin with love, sexuality and personal relationships, apparently the most intimate area of our lives, determined entirely by feelings and quite remote from strategies of calculation and control. Such at least is the picture presented in pop lyrics and pulp fiction, although the reality is rather different. The old church ban on premarital sex has long since crumbled, but now children officially learn in school classes that sex and pregnancy go together, that sexual intercourse carries a danger of AIDS and other infections, that one should therefore 'be careful' in such and such ways. Not everyone sticks to the advice all the time, but everyone has heard through school, the media or public campaigns that there are certain 'risks'. This knowledge has changed ways of dealing with sex and spread new types of planning (from regular use of the pill to the 'just in case' condom in the pocket).

As to long-term relationships, it has meanwhile become evident that in many cases marriage does not keep its promise of being for life. And the more conspicuous the risk of breakdown and divorce, the more strategies of protective cover emerge. Services such as 'premarital therapy' (Leigh 1985), the 'premarital checklist' (Brothers 1985: 63–73) or 'marriage preparation sessions' (Wilkinson 1998: 121) all aim to detect potential flashpoints before the marriage begins for real. There are even a growing number of women who, before getting married, instruct a detective agency to uncover any darker side of their partner's former life (debts, drugs, criminal record, etc.).[4] They want to be sure that their husband-to-be will really make a good husband.

More and more couples draw up a marriage contract covering in detail such points as control over money and assets, the organization of everyday life, and the number of future children. Here too the motive is the same: not to let their happiness simply take its course, but to put it on a secure legal foundation.[5]

Such forms of 'divorce prevention'[6] are not emerging by chance, nor are they merely the product of personal inclination or neurosis. Where everything is uncertain, where old norms and traditions have less and less currency, people want to create commitment, security and reliability in their own private domain (that is, in their personal life as a couple). Here at least they want to make the future calculable.

All this may involve only individual cases, typical only for a minority of people. But, as demographic studies show, another pattern has established itself in recent years which no longer affects just a small group but is tending to become the norm. More and more couples first live together for a time before getting married – or not getting married, as the case may be. It would be quite wrong to explain monocausally the rise of this new lifestyle, as a number of motives are certainly involved. But not for nothing is cohabitation also called a 'trial marriage'; many couples obviously want to see how they get on with each other before wending their way to the registry office (BMJFG 1985: 59; Vaskovics et al. 1991) – a practice that certainly has a logic of its own. When the old assurances provided by the family's selection of potential spouses no longer operate, and when the old images and role models no longer hold up, the range of possible lifestyles and family forms becomes ever broader. And it is precisely then that the idea is thrown up of a practical test before the marriage takes place in earnest. Perhaps this also explains why the population statistics of recent years have been showing a rise in the age of marriage (see table 3.1). Simplifying the picture somewhat, we may say that, when couples must first plan, test and cover themselves, the final decision tends to be taken at a later date.

Whereas in bourgeois society the road to marriage followed a compulsory sequence of events (introduction, parents' approval, engagement, marriage, creation of a household), today the road to living together is quite different. Since formal social restrictions have virtually disappeared, everyone must now create their own safeguards. Out of the range of provisional or experimental forms, everyone can choose what they think is the

Table 3.1   Age at marriage of single men and
women in Germany (in years)

Year	Men	Women
1985	26.6	24.1
1990	27.9	25.5
1993	29.2	26.8
1995	29.7	27.3
1998	30.6	27.8

Source: Compiled from Statistisches Bundesamt (1990:
102), Sommer (1997: 222) and Bundesinstitut für Bevölkerungsforschung (2000: 13)

most sensible mix. Matters thereby come up for decision, and
the outcome depends on each person's earlier relationships,
general formation and life history – not least their previous
experience of relationships. Nowhere is it written that the two
sides will necessarily agree on the answers. Should we move in
together now, later or perhaps not at all? What if she wants to
go to some premarital communication training and he thinks
that's an idiotic waste of time? What if one wants to draw up a
marriage contract and the other sees this as lack of trust; or if
both see the point in a contract but have differing views about
what it should contain? These may be matters for objective
decision, but at issue are also each person's subjective interpretations of particular behaviour, the symbolic content he or she
attaches to it. How necessary is this or that action? If we move
in together, is it just because of the practical and financial
advantages, or does it mean that we're serious about a future
life together? There are no longer any answers that go without
saying, only individual interpretations which, in case of
disagreement, can turn into misunderstandings or even erupt
into mutual reproaches. Approximation by trial and error is
usually the answer, and this may certainly increase the
room for manoeuvre but may well also expand the field of
potential conflict. Giddens is right to point out that our everyday life has become 'experimental', that it involves a 'great

quest' especially in the area of personal relationships (1994a). And as in other kinds of experiment, some succeed and others fail.

Furthermore, the prevailing kinds of safeguard – from a marriage contract to a trial marriage – have an inner logic and hence a dynamic of their own. They are in essence self-protective strategies, which in case of conflict place a premium on the autonomy and the rights of the individual (see chapter 2). But since this makes the stability of the relationship less of a priority, it also increases the risk of its breaking down. Someone who opts for a marriage contract will certainly make their own position more secure if the worst comes to the worst – and will also find it easier to decide on a divorce. Because the costs are lower, they will be able to pull out of the marriage.

Planned parenthood

The population statistics further point to a growing number of 'late parents', especially women, who decide only at a rather advanced age to have their first child (see table 3.2). This trend, too, is certainly not due to one factor alone, but there are good reasons to believe that once again the postponement behaviour involves a desire for protection. In any event, the empirical evidence is that what used to be the most natural thing in the

Table 3.2 Average age of married women at birth of their first child, in West and East Germany, 1970–1998

Year	West Germany	East Germany	Germany
1970	24.3	22.5*	–
1980	25.2	22.3*	–
1991	27.1	24.9	26.9
1995	28.2	26.9	28.1
1998	28.7	27.9	28.7

* Average age of all women at birth of first child.
Sources: Statistisches Bundesamt (1997), Fachserie 1, R1; Bundesinstitut für Bevölkerungsforschung (2000: 13)

world is more and more an undertaking that requires long-term consideration and calculation.

'Family planning' or 'responsible parenthood' (Kaufmann et al. 1988: 122) is the motto of the hour, and the responsibility is measured by a number of factors ranging from relationship stability through income and housing to the time in a working life chosen to have the child. As a result, what is called the time spent deciding is often rather lengthy, especially in the milieu of 'new women' (sometimes also 'new men') who – with many ideas from psychology, childrearing manuals and self-help literature – want to do everything consciously and conscientiously. The programmatic advice given to potential mothers in a women's handbook is: 'think everything through carefully', then 'make a decision you are really sure about' (The Boston Women's Health Book Collective 1987: 640). It is advice which is followed – not always, but to an ever greater extent. One empirical study concludes: 'Many of the female respondents complain of a loss of spontaneity. They feel that children used to be brought into the world more as a matter of course, whereas today women have to make a conscious decision' (BMJFG 1985: 78).

The ubiquitousness of this planning injunction is apparent from the disapproval meted out to those who offend against it. They can expect little sympathy from the public. 'The new morality means conscious, rational, technologically assured contraception. The model is the enlightened modern individual who handles the act of procreation in a responsible spirit. ... Those who make no use of today's unlimited birth control options arouse something akin to suspicion. Contraception is changing from a necessary evil to an enlightened civic duty' (Häussler 1983: 65). New kinds of blame are starting to affect women in particular. When personal wishes and institutional conditions do not tally, the opportunity to plan easily becomes a 'planning trap' (Rerrich 1988: 60); contraceptive technology can then be used to stigmatize women who make the 'wrong' choice or refuse to be 'rational' and 'sensible' in reaching an 'optimal' solution. But the target is only the conduct of individual women, not the contradictory parameters of job and family:

53

it is not the job structures requiring women to make an either–
or choice, but the women who do not want to adapt to such
structures in planning their family, who are treated as 'irrational'. Where the pill and the coil make it possible to conceive of a definite choice for or against a child, the consequences
of 'wrong' decisions become individualized and fall on the
women themselves. (1988: 61)

There are further variants of the planning trap. Women who
put off having children until their job situation is secure may
find when the time comes that other important conditions are
not right – for example, that they do not have, or no longer
have, a stable relationship. And the biological clock keeps
ticking away, making conception and a successful pregnancy
less and less likely. Paradoxically those who plan, postpone
and prevent run the risk of not being able to cash in on all the
planning, if they can no longer have a child when they finally
decide to go ahead.

Prenatal testing and the 'tentative pregnancy'

When the eventual decision to have a child does result in a
pregnancy, the time for planning and precautions is not yet over
– indeed, it is only just beginning. With the rapid growth of
medical technology in the last few decades, especially in relation to human genetics, pregnancy has increasingly become a
risky business involving tests and apparatuses, specialist advice
and intervention, and the many forms of 'care siege' (Frevert
1985). This particularly affects so-called 'risk groups', who
are deemed to present an increased genetic risk (whether because of personal factors such as a relatively advanced age, or
because of a family history pointing to a genetic disorder) and
are therefore strongly recommended to take 'preventative
measures'. What this means in plain language is that, after the
onset of pregnancy (or preferably before), the couple should
seek expert genetic advice, undergo special tests and, if these
are unfavourable, terminate the pregnancy and try again if they
like. The 'tentative pregnancy' has arrived (Rothman 1988).

There are already tendencies to praise behaviour of this kind as expressing a new responsibility, no less. The prominent scientist Hubert Markl, for example, writes: 'To give up having children of one's own for such reasons [genetic risk] deserves to be praised at least as much as, perhaps even more than, the decision to give free rein to a possibly grim fate in a spirit of relentlessly fatalistic piety' (1989). Even clearer is Martin Sass, a prominent presentative of the new bioethics, who considers that high-risk reproductive decisions are 'irresponsible toward the society which takes such severely disabled individuals into its midst' (BMFT 1984: 123). Such views are becoming more common at a more mundane level too, where women who do not take up the offer of prenatal and genetic testing are often treated as selfish, ignorant or stupid: 'They really prefer to stick their head in the sand than to know the truth.'[7]

Today, then, pregnancy is not simply a natural process; it calls for awareness, responsibility and special instruction, and if necessary for genetic advice. This, it is promised, will make possible 'informed reproductive decisions' (Pander et al. 1992: (B)2787). The only question is whether this promise is actually fulfilled; or, to be more precise, when it is fulfilled and when not, and where new dilemmas may arise as a result.

Let us begin with circumstances that pose no particular problem: a couple who want to have a child may be told that, given their family histories, they have no reason to think they face a high genetic risk; or a pregnant woman may be informed that, on the basis of prenatal tests, a particular anomaly (e.g. Down's syndrome) can be ruled out. Such cases are unproblematic because a genetic picture may be drawn which accords with the clients' wishes and hopes; any fears they may have can be cleared away, and their joy at having the child can develop more freely.

The situation is different, however, when the genetic diagnosis permits only a statement of probability (for example, an abnormality risk of 25 per cent for each child). It is well known that such statistical probabilities can never say anything about the particular case, about the pregnancy happening or planned right here and now. But it is also true that 'you can't be a little bit pregnant'. So the quality of the genetic diagnosis does not accord with the situational logic of the decision, which allows of only two possibilities: yes or no, a pregnancy or no pregnancy. Here clients often feel abandoned with their own fears and feelings – not because of any failings on the adviser's part, but because that is how the system works. The knowledge supplied through genetic diagnosis is technically limited knowledge, which cannot address the existential questions and conflicts aroused in the clients.

Greater strain and stress are to be expected when a pregnant woman is informed of something that directly crushes her hopes: that is, when a genetic anomaly is actually established. This faces her with existential questions in the literal sense of the word, questions which concern the life or death of the child growing inside her. More: she herself must *actively decide* whether it lives or not, if necessary giving her consent to its death. On the one side is her fear of the child's future suffering and handicap, as well as of the effects on her own life; on the other side are feelings of guilt, fear of causing death, mourning for a child who (as is often case with older women) has for long been her dearest wish.

The aim of human genetics is to help clients achieve greater autonomy in their lives. But, in the tragic cases just described, things look rather different from the patient's point of view. Many feel thrown into a situation which, whatever decision they make, is charged with fear and guilt (Ringler 1994; Schmidt et al. 1994). Many suddenly find themselves caught in a 'double bind', where none of the courses open to them is what they want. In an academic book on the practice and principles of genetic consultation, Angus Clarke writes:

> individuals or couples making reproductive decisions in the face of a risk of genetic disease often experience their predicament as being a no-win situation; they can live with the sadness of childlessness; they can take a chance, and risk having a child (perhaps a second child) affected by a cruel disease, with the sorrow and suffering this may cause; or they can decide to

subject a pregnancy to prenatal diagnosis, and perhaps to terminate the pregnancy if the test result is unfavourable. (1994: 3)

No one can deny that these are decisions. But it is equally
obvious that they are tragic decisions. Prenatal diagnosis can
certainly reveal things to patients, but the questions that may
then suddenly loom up touch on quite different aspects. What
is life? How is its value to be measured? Whose needs and rights
come first in case of doubt? Whose must go under? As a
popular introduction to prenatal diagnosis put it: a 'moral odyssey' begins at this point (Blatt 1991: 9).

It only remains to ask what this entails for the couple. For in
the end there are two, a man and a woman, whose child or wish
to have a child is at stake. As we know from social psychology,
emergency situations can have the positive effect of bringing
people closer together, around the questions they have in
common but perhaps also in common suffering. But the effect
may also be negative, dividing and separating the couple. It is a
feature of an odyssey that no one can say which is the right
direction, and so different individuals may arrive at different
views about the direction they want to take on their trial-and-
error path. Conflicts between partners have never been systematically investigated, but the available material suggests that the
woman and the man are by no means always of the same view
about the issue of prenatal diagnosis (e.g. Clarke 1994: 3;
Richards 1996: 264; Wolff and Jung 1994: 8). So what happens
if he is in favour of testing and she is against, or vice versa?
Perhaps the man has strong ties to the church and rules out
testing because he is fundamentally opposed to abortion,
whereas the woman, with her gynaecologist's words about
multiple risk factors ringing in her ears, is more inclined to go
ahead, because 'it's better to be cautious, especially at my late
age.' What then?

Then various authorities clash with one another – religious
teachings versus modern experts – and the couple have to sort it
out for themselves. The question becomes particularly explosive, because no amount of attention to the other's arguments
and no amount of patient consideration can reduce the

starkness of the either–or replies. Here there is no middle way, no half-test or semi-termination of the pregnancy. It is probably true that in most cases the couple eventually reach some kind of compromise, but for some there may be a lasting residue of resentment and misunderstanding. One sees how the techno-logical options, while promising greater autonomy and freedom of choice, may unleash a particular dynamic in a couple. Spiral-ling pressures to make a decision may, as it were, slip their way into the life of the family.

Medical technology from the beginning to the end of life

It would be wrong to think that these are special cases applic-able only to older couples. For, with the rapid decoding of the human genetic map, more and more biological predispositions are becoming visible and potentially open to medical interven-tion and regulation. Individual genetic profiles make it possible to say who is especially at risk and in which area, to issue recommendations and warnings on matters ranging from diet, work and choice of partner through to holiday destination, sporting activity and hobbies. (In certain groups of the popula-tion, the results of genetic testing are already among the criteria affecting choice of partner.[8]) As genetic dispositions are always operating – in every branch of medicine from cardiac and circulatory disorders to cancer, allergies and diabetes – everyone becomes a risk-bearer of one kind or another. 'There is no longer anyone unaffected' (Müller-Neumann and Langenbu-cher 1991: 11). Someone who is in good health today may suddenly be faced with a decision in relation to intensive medi-cine or an organ transplant – perhaps for himself or herself, perhaps for a dying parent, a partner injured in a car crash, or a child involved in an accident while playing. Reference points that once appeared to be constants of human existence become variable through the development of medical technology. As Giddens sums it up: 'The body is becoming a phenomenon of choices and actions' (1991: 8).

Consequently an ever greater number of conscious decisions need to be made, at the most diverse levels, in answer to the question: How do we want to shape our lives? This also concerns the basic question so dramatically affected by the new intensive and reproductive medicine: What is human life itself? When does it begin, how should its end be defined? What used to be fixed by 'nature', or else determined by religious precepts, is today (when even legal restrictions are unclear in the field of medicine) increasingly left for the citizen to anticipate and plan in time as his or her own responsibility. Let us take a couple of examples. One common recommendation in the field of medical technology is that everyone should think of a worst-case scenario and decide in advance whether they would consent to an organ transplant, or that they should make it clear in writing whether all the possibilities of intensive medicine should be used in their own case. Since the existence of various criteria for death may cause mistrust among potential organ donors, a scientific journal recently proposed that 'every person should declare during their lifetime when they wish to be considered dead': when their heart stops beating, when their brain shuts down, or when they lose consciousness without hope of recovery.[9] Some time ago, the case of a brain-dead pregnant woman hit the headlines in Germany, and after heated controversy a legal recommendation was made that 'a pregnant woman, after being suitably informed', should declare whether in the event of her brain death she wishes her residual functions to be artificially restored until the foetus is capable of surviving without her (Heuermann 1994: 139).

Can such questions ever be answered in advance? And what happens if someone is unable (or unwilling) to answer them? In extreme cases, the relatives are then faced with what one might call 'impossible decisions'. They are decisions that essentially no one can make, no one can take responsibility for – what definite rules could there be for judging on life and death? – and yet they have to be made whether anyone likes it or not. The central problem is what should be done by way of operations and radiotherapy, invasive surgery and technological applications, artificial feeding and artificial respiration? How much and for how long? Each of these questions comes down to the one awe-inspiring alternative: to allow someone to live or to die. In

Patrimony: A True Story, the American writer Philip Roth gives an account of the choices faced during the last years of his father's life, right up to the final hours when matters of life and death were not in the hands of fate but required a conscious decision.

> ... when I arrived at the hospital emergency room to which he had been rushed from his bedroom at home, I was confronted by an attending physician prepared to take 'extraordinary measures' and to put him on a breathing machine. Without it there was no hope, though, needless to say – the doctor added – the machine wasn't going to reverse the progress of the tumor, which appeared to have begun to attack his respiratory function. The doctor also informed me that, by law, once my father had been hooked up to the machine he would not be disconnected, unless he could once again sustain breathing on his own. A decision had to be made immediately and, since my brother was still en route by plane from Chicago, by me alone.
>
> And I, who had explained to my father the provisions of the living will and got him to sign it, didn't know what to do. How could I say no to the machine if it meant that he needn't continue to endure this agonizing battle to breathe? How could I take it on myself to decide that my father should be finished with life, life which is ours to know just once? Far from invoking the living will, I was nearly on the verge of ignoring it and saying, 'Anything! Anything!' (Roth 1992: 232)

Decisions such as this always contain, explicitly or implicitly, what Giddens calls 'life politics' (which he again and again illustrates with reference to human genetics and reproductive medicine). The conclusion is generally applicable: 'The "end of nature" opens up many new issues for consideration.... Life-political issues ... call for a remoralizing of social life' (Giddens 1991: 224). Even in the lowly spheres of everyday life where the normal citizen is called upon to act, dramatic situations can suddenly arise and require decisions that are anything but simple. Since in many cases there is not just one morally fault-less answer, each decision tends to bring with it distinctive problems that often involve incalculable risks and burdens. Here suffering must be weighed against suffering, life against life; abstract statistics and probabilities must be converted into existential judgements (let Father have more treatment or allow him to die – what is reasonable, and for whom?). The individual is caught in a dilemma which can hardly be resolved: 'The capability of adopting freely chosen lifestyles, a fundamental benefit generated by a post-traditional order, stands in tension, not only with barriers to emancipation, but with a variety of moral dilemmas. No one should underestimate how difficult it will be to deal with these' (1991: 231).

It should be added that these moral dilemmas become especially sharp when, as is most common with medical technology, they concern several people each with their own interests and rights, life plans and values. It is necessary to weigh these up and to reach an understanding – but can that be done? Not all members of families are harmonious, patient and loving with one another, nor are their motives always high-minded. What was true of prenatal diagnosis applies here *a fortiori*, in the sense that it concerns an additional number of persons. Situations can well be imagined where husband opposes wife, mother opposes son, or brother and sister disagree with each other over whether certain medical-technological options should be employed: for example, over whether Father should be put on an artificial respirator; or whether a severely handicapped newborn child should be given intensive medical treatment; or whether one family member should take the Huntington's disease test, even though its result would also reveal the genetic fate of the others. What happens in these cases if each family member has access to different information or advice (from television or self-help groups, or from different doctors, therapists and clergymen)? For wars of religion or belief can also break out over 'life politics', reaching deep inside the family. In this sense, the new confusion that marks the realm of the personal in the contemporary world does not only affect relationships between men and women, parents and children. It is also a new confusion on moral issues, on the sometimes impossible decisions and conflicts that we have to face.

Unplanned consequences of the planning project

It has so far been argued that life in modernity has increasingly become a planning project. This means first of all that we are living in 'the age of clever people', as Giddens puts it; that expert knowledge, conveyed especially through the media and popular science, is entering ever more spheres of our everyday life. The finding, filtering and processing of information is a routine requirement. Those who cannot keep up – because they lack the cognitive (or, in the case of foreign immigrants, linguistic) requisites, or because other demands do not leave them with enough time – are poor in information, sometimes in a quite literal sense. Anyone who does not have the skill to calculate, combine and manoeuvre in the jungle of insurance premiums, tax rates and railway fares, anyone who does not study tables, compare information and switch around among suppliers, will end up paying over the odds. It would appear, then, that those whose education, background and other resources give them a better understanding of things will be able to extend their lead in life, whereas those who started out with little to show for themselves will tend to lose more ground as time goes by.

But more is involved here than just surfing between various tax rates and building society schemes, or working out the best cost–benefit ratio. In the age of growing individualization, each individual is more and more faced with the question of how to develop and protect their family relationships so that they do not suddenly suffer injury in the field of experimentation. This applies not least to health matters – from birth (or rather conception) right through to death. With the rapid development of medical technology, what used to be 'nature' is fanning out into an ever greater number of individual options. And, as we have seen, the spiral of decision twists its way deep into the family. The more options that high-tech medicine offers – and it would be easy to find examples from other spheres – the more likely it becomes that different members of a family will have different views about the right direction to take, not only in the choice of muesli brands or car makes, but in morally delicate matters that are of literally vital importance.

Everyday life, then, develops to the accompaniment of a host of major and minor decisions. These form a kind of ongoing programme that leads people into a jungle of information and not infrequently produces a new sense of disorientation, requiring 'optimum' solutions because everyone today must produce their own economic and social safeguards. All this constitutes the undercurrent of irritation, disquiet and exasperation which is a basic part of the experience of modernity.

The planning mentality characteristic of contemporary life is thus not merely an expression of personal inclinations, compulsions or neuroses; it is not an individual mania or a mystery virus that has suddenly infected more and more people. Rather, it is part of the global project of modernity, exhibiting as it does the new plasticity of life with its associated opportunities, checks and pressures. Here as in other spheres – partnership and parenthood, education, job choice, consumption, and so on – everyday activity faces new demands as the temporal horizon becomes broader and longer. The present is more and more 'forced into the future'.

Of course, there is a reverse side to this new breadth of choice. Planning gives rise to a planning trap, as prevention does to a prevention trap. If we think this through a little, it becomes clear that individuals today no longer have to contend only with accidents and mishaps. More typically, they must be forearmed against the 'side-effects' thrown up in the very process of forearming, so that they do not themselves become hopelessly entangled in the acts of checking, calculating and preventing. Individuals have to be careful, but they must also be careful about their very carefulness. Life in the individualized society is thus a risky business, a highly complicated balancing act. To quote Giddens once again: 'The more we try to colonize the future, the more likely it is to spring surprises upon us' (1994b: 58).

4

Generational Contract and Gender Relations

When the new women's movement sprang up in the late sixties to early seventies, the relationship between the sexes came back into the public field of vision. Lives and expectations that had been running on the more or less clearly defined tracks of 'gender roles' now began to branch out more widely. Relations between men and women, including not least relations of misunderstanding and dependence, were no longer just the material of private conversation or conflict but excited the attention of the media, politicians and public opinion. Whether the inequality between the sexes was a fact of nature or a politically objectionable product of society, whether equality was possible and desirable and, if so, how it should be achieved – these were questions which ensured a veritable explosion of debate.

In the 1980s, although discussion on these themes was by no means ended – and although the issues associated with them had been neither clarified nor resolved – a further question began to detach itself from the horizon of the merely private. Now the relationship between the generations came under scrutiny. As falling birth-rates combined with rising life expectancy to define the contours of the 'ageing society' in the public mind, old certainties began to crumble and new issues and fears to be articulated. There were arguments about pension guarantees, bitter disputes over the forms of long-term nursing care, and much debate about the financial burdens on society that would develop with the changing age structure. The relationship between old and young people, both quantitative and qualitative, became a topic for political commissions, academic studies and population forecasts. Issues to do with justice, distributive justice between the generations, also came to the fore. Can the welfare state still provide for the needs and situations of the different generations? If resources become tight, as they are expected to do, whose needs and claims should take priority, whose will have to be scaled down and made less secure?

In the years since the 1980s, these themes of relations between the sexes and between the generations have lost none of their explosiveness, and there is still much public talk of both. But, at least until a short time ago, the discussions were conducted separately: 'men and women' over here, 'old and young people' over there. This is a mistake, because it does not allow important causes and effects to be grasped. In this chapter I shall therefore develop an approach that lays bare the interaction between the two themes. I shall ask what the relationship between the generations and the relationship between the sexes have to do with each other. Is it a historical accident that both are no longer treated as a matter of course, that both are sure to cause agitation among the public? Or are the two associated with and dependent upon each other in a number of ways?

Traditional expectations: women as a 'hidden resource' in relations between the generations

One of the premises of the relationship between the generations is that periods of autonomy and dependence alternate in the human life span. First there is the infant, totally reliant upon the support of others; then the healthy adult, who can organize his or her life independently; and finally the elderly person, who is again reliant upon the help of others – perhaps only occasionally for some little everyday tasks, perhaps in the larger sense of round-the-clock care. It should be added, of course, that 'others' is here a vague and loose term, because what is really meant is not at all gender-neutral. In our society it is above all women who are responsible for support tasks in the relationship between the generations – both for the care of children at the beginning of life, and for the care of the elderly at its end.

Childcare is women's work

In the industrial heartlands of the West, equality of rights has become a generally accepted value in gender relations, yet this value is still far from being realized in everyday life. As many studies have shown, for various countries but especially clearly in the case of Germany, it is in relation to childcare that the greatest barriers and obstacles are erected. Take, for example, the results of a representative survey conducted by Metz-Göckel and Müller (1985: 26–7): 'When asked how a family with children.... can best divide up the tasks of outside work, housekeeping and childrearing, the great majority of German men cite the model in which the woman stays at home and the man goes out to work.... Men see this not as discrimination against women but as something in the nature of things.' The authors comment on this as follows: 'The women's question has become the child question, the problem of private childcare. Nowhere else in our study did we come up against such a stable male bastion. Men stubbornly insist on the irreplaceability of the mother and in this way.... on their own freedom from childcare work' (1985: 81).

The invocation of children – is this a last attempt by men to hang on to their privileges? It may well seem so – and yet this is only part of the story. For, as other studies show, the idea that caring for and bringing up the children is mainly the mother's task is also common among women.[1] (These studies also show, however, that most women would welcome a more flexible division of labour and would especially like men to take part in the work side of childcare, not only in the fun and leisure aspects.) Women are caught here in a basic dilemma. In a large-scale survey conducted by the German Youth Institute on the

66

theme 'Child? Job? Or both?', we read: 'Women today have a clear orientation to work outside the home, but they can only really live it out at a secondary level. What holds them back are the children' (Erler et al. 1988b: 31). The authors then comment:

> The results of the study show that a job outside the home has indeed become the model for women, but that … in the eyes both of women themselves and of the surrounding world … any job would worsen their quality as mothers. … This is an ideological trap, a 'surreptitious' dual message, which makes women increasingly unsure of themselves at every stage in their lives. (Erler et al. 1988b: 12)

So much for the attitudes of men and women. Their daily behaviour points in the same direction. More recently, it is true, there have been studies of fathers with a part-time job and househusbands (e.g. Strümpel et al. 1988), including all manner of media reports in which the new man presents life with baby as an exciting experience.[2] It is also undoubtedly true that younger men involve themselves in bringing up children far more than their fathers and grandfathers did. Nevertheless, in this generation too, men are far less active than women in the realm of childcare. Take parental leave, for instance. Here men are a tiny minority indeed: figures for Germany show that, of those taking parental leave, 98 per cent are women and fewer than 2 per cent are men. Or take single parents.[3] Here the proportion of men, that is, single fathers, has risen to 16.5 per cent.[4] But on closer examination we find that, compared with single mothers, they look after fewer children on average and that the children they do look after are older, more independent and less demanding of care (Dorbritz 1993–4; Schwartz 1993–4). In the more typical family unit, a recent study by the German Federal Statistical Office has shown: 'Economically active married women … spend more than twice as much time as economically active men on the care of their offspring under six, while married women who are not economically active outside the home [spend] more than three times as much' (BMFSFJ and Statistisches Bundesamt 1995).

The work of raising children is thus still mainly the task of women, especially of mothers and not infrequently, we should add, of grandmothers. Childcare fits into a web of solidarity stretching across three generations – from child to mother to grandmother. As the results of an EU study have shown, in most countries of the European Union it is mainly grandmothers who look after the children when young mothers go out to work (Rerrich 1993: 331; see also BMFSFJ 1997: 133–4 and BMJFFG 1986: 84ff), and, even more, who step in on occasions such as school holidays or emergencies such as the mother's illness (BMJFFG 1986: 85ff; Rerrich 1993: 328ff).

Care of the elderly is women's work

Let us begin by glancing back at pre-industrial society, where different generations lived closer together than they do today. This past is often nostalgically idealized as in a Victorian painting: grandmother at the spinning wheel, grandfather in the armchair, a merry crowd of children at their feet, everything pervaded by an aroma of baked apples. Here as elsewhere, however, the legend of an idyllic past is delusory; in reality, the pre-industrial family was mainly a union born of necessity and compulsion, held together by much work and threatening fate (bad weather, plunder, famine). For the sake of survival, it was the material interests of the farm and village, not the freedom of the individual, which took priority; little room was left for personal consideration, tenderness and empathy with others. And the strong social cohesion, praised in later times as an example of love of one's neighbour, stemmed mainly from an awareness of mutual dependence (Borscheid 1988).

Since those times, the ways in which people live have fundamentally changed. Industrialization brought with it the rise of the bourgeois family, which was supposed to be primarily a community of feeling rather than of work. This form too, as we have long known, is not a locus of pure love and harmony; it produces its own frictions, irritations and conflicts. Yet, for all its defects, it is also a source of mutual support that is felt across the generations. Certainly there are some neglected old people, shunted off into a home, who have no one to care about them. Some suffer from loneliness and isolation, some have only defective daily care and provision. But for the majority the family is an important – indeed, the most important – support they have in life. As studies have shown, in Germany the emotional and everyday practical support of old people, and any necessary personal care and attention, are still provided mainly within the family. And, once again, a clear gender distribution lies behind the general term 'family'; it is above all wives, daughters and granddaughters who perform the care work for the older generation (BMJFFG 1986: 154ff; BMFS 1994: 191ff). Even when professional helpers stand in, they tend to be female, as it is mainly women who work in the caring professions.

Women living under constant pressure

If it is still mainly women who look after children and the elderly as well as doing most of the housework, and if more and more women have been going out to work in recent decades, how is this combination possible? The answer, roughly speaking, is that women have taken on an extra burden – which has its price, especially for women, in the shape of constant everyday pressure. It is not only their joie de vivre which suffers, not only their nerves and energy, but to a massive extent also their actual health. Under such conditions, chronic fatigue is not the exception but the rule – what is aptly known as 'hurry sickness'. From the vast amount of material, here are just a couple of examples.

In a book on working parents with the revealing title *The Second Shift*, the American sociologist Arlie Hochschild showed from empirical evidence that although men 'helped' with the children – some more, some less – women suffered from a striking 'leisure gap' (Hochschild and Machung 1989: 4). In the interview material, they reported feeling exhausted and torn apart, sickly and emotionally drained; they kept obsessively circling round the theme of sleep (how many hours they needed, how much their women friends needed, why they never got enough). Hochschild tersely comments: 'These women talked about sleep the way a hungry person talks about food' (1989: 9). Not by chance does she begin the book with a chapter entitled 'A speed-up in the family'. This shows that, in families where both parents are economically active and suffer growing pressure:

> working mothers are its primary victims. It is ironic, then, that often it falls to women to be the 'time and motion' expert of family life. Watching inside homes, I noticed it was often the mother who rushed children, saying, 'Hurry up! It's time to go', 'Finish your cereal now', 'You can do that later', 'Let's go!' ... Often a younger child will rush out ... while the older ... stalls, resistant, sometimes resentful: 'Mother is always rushing us.' Sadly enough, women are more often the lightning rods for family aggressions aroused by the speed-up of work and family life. They are the 'villains' in a process of which they are also the primary victims. (1989: 9–10)

The American journalist Ellen Goodman raises similar points – only she goes even further, not just establishing facts but consciously questioning and provoking. Several of her articles deal with the post-war baby-boomers, who today are trying somehow to combine a job with looking after children and elderly parents. One story concerns her own experience. When her mother wanted to move into smaller accommodation because of her age, she went to help her sort through her belongings. Being in her usual rush, she wanted to do this as quickly but also as practically and efficiently as possible; only gradually did she begin to listen to her mother, who told the story of each object, the memories associated with it, the feelings it evoked. Then she realized that her much-practised efficiency was here quite out of place:

> Finally seeing this, I shift gears. I slow down and sit down. And doing so, I realize how easy it is to speed through important moments without even noticing.
>
> I have a friend whose mother says with good humor that our whole generation should wear T-shirts that read, 'Gotta Go.' We are forever in a rush. We do drive-by visits.

They call us the 'sandwich generation', because so many of us are caught between parents and children, work and home. But maybe we're named after the one item on the menu meant to be eaten on the run.

It's not just the tasks of life that we rush through. Not just the cleaning, the shopping, the commuting. We also manage emotions with one foot on the running board. We even shortcut the experiences of life....

It made me think of Carly Simon's ironic song about our times:

> 'Make love in the microwave
> Think of all the time you save.'[5]

Or again: 'We talked about the sense of channel-surfing through life. Work, click, kids, click, parents, click, errands, click. ... What happens when life becomes a list? When even the pleasurable things become items to check off' (Goodman 1996: 9).

Hochschild and Goodman write about women at different stages of life and the family cycle, but the pictures they draw are similar. The awareness of life that women are left with – at least in the family's more intensive periods – is mainly a matter of short commands: Hurry up! Get a move on! Just coming! I've got to go now!

The times are changing: women as a 'scarce resource' in relations between the generations

Up until now, as we have seen, it has mainly been women who have looked after children and the elderly, carrying out the routine tasks that give cohesion to relations between the generations. But will this still be the case tomorrow? Should we expect that women will continue to do this work, or will they increasingly adopt different lifestyles?

Childcare used to be a comparatively easy task, routinely carried out among most sections of the population without any great need for special instruction, but as we draw closer to the present day it becomes subject to more and more demands

71

and requirements. Under modern conditions of social mobility – so we hear from countless advice books, magazines or courses for parents – it is now obligatory to give the new generation 'the best possible start in life'. At the same time, however, highly industrialized modern societies display in many areas a 'structural hostility to children' (Kaufmann et al. 1995: 169ff): that is to say, their basic structures do not fit the needs, the rhythm or the compulsive restlessness of young children (think, for example, of housing construction, road traffic or the toxins in the air and food). On the one hand, the best possible start in life; on the other hand, structural hostility: those who are responsible for children must constantly operate within this contradiction, find ways of compensating and striking a balance, negotiate and adjudicate, mediate among various fronts, stave off the worst time after time. In this situation, so fraught with consequences, work for children has expanded into a complex performance acted out among resistances of the most diverse kind (Beck-Gernsheim 1989: 111ff).

Who, then, will do the work? Up to now it has mainly been women. But in the last few decades changes in education and at work, as well as in the family cycle, the legal system, and so on, have set in train far-reaching changes in what counts as a normal female biography. As a result, more and more women have been at least partially released from the ties of family; they can expect less and less to be provided for by a husband, and are forced to become – often inconsistently, of course – independent and self-supporting. In other words, they experience the demand and the pressure for 'a life of their own'. This leaves little space, time, nerves and energy for 'living for others', not least for the ever-expanding demands of childcare.

Contrary to a widespread misunderstanding, this does not mean that in the course of women's liberation children have become less important to women. Indeed, in individualized society (with its high degree of anonymity, division of labour, geographical and social mobility), the desire for children may even become stronger and more significant, as part of a quest for meaning, recognition, rootedness, and so on (Beck-Gernsheim 1997a). What is true is that women are increasingly caught in a dilemma, since there are inadequate facilities for them to combine job and family, and they get only limited help from men with the children. The outcome is a historically new constellation, in which many women have a strong desire for children but, if they act on this wish, have to reckon with considerable costs for their own life in terms of limited job opportunities, excessive daily workloads, reduced leisure, financial insecurity in old age, and a risk of poverty in the event of divorce. Studies from Germany provide graphic evidence of this dilemma.

When young women are asked about their ideas and plans for life, most of them still say that they want to have children (Schwartz 1994; Pohl 1995). Yet, as the statistical data show, this wish is increasingly deferred until later in life. Often it is also reduced, so that women who would like to have had two or more children end up having only one. And in quite a few cases the wish is first deferred and then abandoned. Among younger age groups there has been a marked rise in the number of women who go through life without having a child. In Britain: 'According to official government forecasts at least 20 per cent of women born in the 1960s will not have children, rising to nearly one quarter of those who were born in the 1970s' (Franks 1999: 197–8). And in Germany the trend is even more pronounced (see figure 4.1): of women born in 1965, approximately 31 per cent in West Germany and 26 per cent in East Germany will remain childless (Dorbritz and Gärtner 1999: 14–15).

The situation is especially striking in eastern Germany, where birth-rates plummeted in the early years after unification.[6] As many of the former policies making it possible to combine work and family were discontinued, women learned that motherhood now sharply reduced their chances in the labour market and that single mothers, in particular, were being forced more and more to the sidelines. It suddenly became clear that from then on children would be a professional, social and financial risk to their own lives; that what had once appeared a matter of course – the combination of children with other goals in life, especially a job – was now fragile and open to doubt. As recent surveys have shown, most young women in eastern Germany

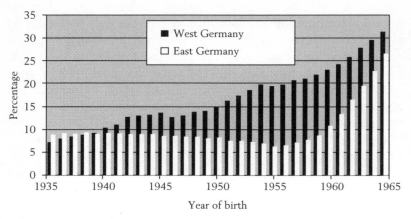

Figure 4.1 Percentage of women born between 1935 and 1965 who remained childless
Source: Dorbritz and Gärtner (1999: 14)

do still want to have children; the new thing they are learning is that they must go about it more circumspectly, through gradual approximations, as it were. One might say that a social-historical experiment is here being conducted before our eyes, in the course of which the wish to have children suddenly becomes the 'children question' requiring careful consideration and calculation on the part of individuals.

But are not grandmothers still a 'hidden reserve' in childcare, as we described earlier? They still are, of course. But whether they will still be in the future is quite another question. One empirical study has already shown examples of the 'at least partial refusal of grandmothers to work' (Rerrich 1993: 331): that is, they are glad to help out with the grandchildren but only for clearly defined periods, not as a flexible reserve on call all the time. This is hardly surprising. For the change in what counts as a normal female biography produces not only new women and new mothers, but also new grandmothers. Many women now in their early fifties (and, even more, women who will reach that age in the next few decades) already carry the 'virus' of hopes, or at least some ideas, of a life of their own. They have their own aims beyond the radius of the family –

whether a job of their own, or voluntary work of some kind, or (finally!) the pursuit of their own interests. Should they give all this up to help out as a babysitter and granny-on-duty for the next generation? In this too women are less prepared to take things on. To quote the above-mentioned study (1993: 331): 'Grandmothers willing to take over at any and every time... will presumably become an ever scarcer resource.' And, as one social scientist has said, the situation of today's working mothers is comparatively simple, because women who are now grandmothers are mostly housewives; this will certainly change as more of tomorrow's older women enter the labour market. The general conclusion, then, must be that it will not become easier for the next generation of women to combine a job with a family – on the contrary, the problems will increase and become 'much more acute' (Liebau 1996: 21).

Who will help out in old age?

In the last few decades, life expectancy has risen quite sharply. This means that the number of people reaching a great and very great age is increasing and will continue to increase. There will be more eighty- and ninety-year-olds (see tables 4.1, 4.2 and 4.3).

Table 4.1   Numbers of people aged 80 or more in Germany (West and East)

Year	Number
1950	695,400
1960	1,158,800
1975	1,734,800
1995	3,238,000*
2015	3,948,000*
2030	4,347,000*

* These numbers are projections.
Source: Author's calculation from the report of the Bundesinstitut für Bevölkerungsforschung, *Die Alten der Zukunft* (1993), appendix, tables 12b and 16

Table 4.2   Estimated population aged 85 and over, England and Wales

Year	Number
1948	197,000
1998	1,016,700

Source: Office for National Statistics

Table 4.3   Age structure of the projected population, 1996–2036, England and Wales, in thousands

Year	Age 85–89	Age 90 and over
1950	659	311
2006	690	404
2016	764	466
2026	895	506
2036	1,270	758

Source: Office for National Statistics

The media and advertising are filled with images of the 'youthful old' – fit and active, mobile and energetic, today in the gym, tomorrow perhaps in Majorca. The picture is not entirely false, but even less is it entirely correct. For it suppresses the other side of old age: the situation of the 'elderly old'. As chronic or degenerative diseases make themselves felt to a greater extent in older age groups, the extra years are for many bound up with deteriorating health – years when it is no longer possible to be fully independent, and when the remaining physical, mental and social resources must largely be devoted to the body's sheer survival. The consequences are predictable. The growth in life expectancy is rapidly increasing the number of people who, no longer strong enough to look after themselves, have to rely upon many forms of support and, if necessary, on comprehensive nursing care.

So who will carry out the work of care and support? According to various studies, it is doubtful whether the daughters and daughters-in-law of future generations will be either able or willing to do it (*Zwischenbericht* 1994: 158; Rosenkranz 1996). Most likely, women will continue to feel responsible for the well-being of their parents and parents-in-law and provide them with emotional support, as well as helping on occasions with everyday tasks. Being, however, faced with the demands and pressures of a life of their own, they will be less able (perhaps also less willing) to offer day-to-day support and time-consuming care.

Furthermore, the fragility of the traditional model evidently affects the role of the family in providing care and support for its sick as well as elderly members (Badura 1981). This applies especially to the handling of illness in old age: 'the crucial factor in how people live once their health begins to fail is not so much their age as the presence or absence of family members in the household ... or in the immediate vicinity' (Kytir and Münz 1991). But when different lifestyles increasingly appear along-side the so-called traditional family, when the number of single, childless, divorced and cohabiting people is on the rise, it is an open question how they will be cared for in old age. Alternative lifestyles may offer advantages in many respects, by freeing individuals from the family straitjacket and allowing them greater freedom of choice (this being the reason, in some cases anyway, why people opt for alternative lifestyles). But as yet it is completely unclear how such constellations will shape up in their old age, some thirty or forty years from now. We may perhaps offer some speculations.

Many relationships will by then belong to a more or less distant past, and a 'part-life companion' will by definition hardly be likely to become a companion in old age. Other types of relationship may prove to be less practical, less capable of functioning in the later years of life. For example, couples who live in separate dwellings, perhaps even in separate towns, face problems as soon as their radius of mobility declines, as soon as it becomes more difficult for them to get out and about. For couples without children the turning-point will come when one partner dies and the survivor (usually the woman) is left alone. In the case of divorced families, if contact with the father or the paternal grandparents has completely broken down, support for them is hardly likely to be forthcoming in the physical and perhaps mental frailty of old age. For, although their children and grandchildren are related to them by blood, they are otherwise largely strangers without the emotional bonds that might result in care support.

It is sometimes said that friendship networks may provide security in old age and help in case of need, that such networks may even develop as the family of the future. This may be true, at least in favorable circumstances, but a more cautious answer may come to mind if one compares the mechanisms underlying friendship with those of the traditional family: namely, common origin in the latter, affection and personal choice in the former. The cohesion offered by the traditional family is by no means simply a matter of love; it often comes from a sense of duty, instilled through moral pressure, social expectations and the pangs of conscience. Friendship, on the other hand, must keep itself going without duty or external pressure; it is free and voluntary and therefore (at least potentially) a less durable bond; its strength is at the same time its weakness. In any event, as it represents a more open kind of bond, more has to be done to preserve it. It must be maintained and looked after, or else it will slowly wither away.

There is also a kind of biological or physical limit to the potential of friendship in old age. In contrast to the traditional family made up of individuals from several generations, friends gained through school, work or leisure activity are mostly similar in age to one another – which means that, when one friend is in need of help and care, the other's powers are also often failing and are anyway hardly sufficient to give more than occasional support to someone living in another place (perhaps another district or even town). Constant help, perhaps round-the-clock care, would clearly be asking too much (Hradil 1995a: 154).

A comparison between the family and friendship networks in old age therefore results in a complex picture. Clearly it would be too one-sided to note only the decay of traditional institutions and family forms, not the early signs of friendship networks that are appearing in certain groups of society. One has to be aware of the limitations of such networks, however, for they require a certain level of autonomy and independence to be successful. Without being either alarmist or over-optimistic, one will then realize, as one study of personal help in old age put it, that 'each individual must increasingly construct his or her social integration and emergency safety-nets'. Such nets have holes in them, of course, and 'many of the less active and less socially competent... will remain left out' (Diewald 1993: 751 ff).

The growing need for care amid unclear responsibilities

The previous considerations point to a diagnosis of the following kind. As regards care of the elderly, we see *both* a dramatic rise in the need for support *and* a decline in the number of people who take responsibility for providing it as a matter of course (whether out of conscience or duty or social expectations). The scissors are opening ever wider between 'needs' and 'personnel'.[7] The conclusion here is thus strikingly similar to the case of childcare: in both areas there are huge 'gaps in supply'. Or, as a recent German government report on the family puts it:

> In future, the tasks of care and support for old people that fall on families will become even greater and more difficult than they already are. The same social trends that affect childcare are also taking definite shape in relation to care for the elderly: the circle of immediate family from which support and even care for an older member can generally be expected will become still more limited. At the same time, the spatial mobility and remoteness of family members will grow ... which means that there will be ever fewer persons who stand in a strong family relationship, including care responsibilities, towards elderly people in need of daily or possibly basic assistance. (BMFS 1994: 193)

Now, precisely in view of the fragility of the traditional family, there is an increasing tendency to rely upon professional assistance. But the limits of this model also soon become

79

apparent, not least because of the previously mentioned trend that women who work in the caring professions (and it is mainly women) have already undergone the change in what counts as a normal female biography. As survey results have shown, instead of sacrificing themselves they increasingly want a private life, free time and family of their own, and therefore a job like others in which there are regular hours, finishing times and paid holidays (Dunkel 1993). They no longer think of their work in terms of patient service, but expect from it an independent and skilled sphere of activity with opportunities for further training, promotion and a reasonable income (Rabe-Kleberg 1993). With the changing pattern of women's lives, a structural change has already taken place in the caring professions and it will become even deeper in years to come. What sociologist Ilona Ostner wrote in another context also applies here: the special work orientation of women is 'becoming a scarce resource' (1992: 120). The study from which we have already quoted draws the same conclusion:

> The handling of problems associated with people in need of care and assistance has hitherto been [left] to the work morality of women who care for family members or do such work as their profession. So long as the traditional model of integration through duty and self-denial continued to guide women's behaviour ... such a form of social organization of care could still function. ... Now, however, the social conditions have changed and will change still further. ... Duty and self-denial will no longer be automatically offered by the younger generation of women. ... We can thus see more clearly the limits of any solution to the problem of care which takes for granted women's living-for-others in both the professional and the private sphere. (Dunkel 1993)

Demographic change, transformation of the normal female biography, fragility of the traditional family – these are all keywords to evoke how the situation of elderly people may look in the future and how they will be cared for. In sum, all the developments we have been discussing point to one simple question: 'Who will care for us in old age?' (Kytir and Münz 1991).

The search for new models

Women's labour capacity, it has been argued, is becoming a scarce resource in the relationship between the generations, with the result that care gaps have appeared for both children and the elderly. So what is to be done? In the social policy debate, a number of different proposals have been put forward.

First, some continue to look especially to women in their search for model solutions. If women moved away from 'exaggerated individualism' and back towards the family, we are told, then the problem would be solved. This is the drift of the argument in *The War over the Family: Capturing the Middle Ground* (1983), by the American sociologists Brigitte Berger and Peter Berger, and similar propositions are well known in Britain too. But their prospects of success are rather slim, precisely because they are based upon misconceptions about both the past and the present. With regard to the past, such authors cultivate the dream of a perfect world of our ancestors – a dream long since refuted by historical research. They take no account of the fact that family life in earlier times had a distinctly dark side, ruthlessly expressed in the way in which its weaker members (women as well as children and the elderly) were treated (see e.g. Borscheid 1988). As for the present, such recipes fail to appreciate the changes that have taken place in the normal female biography – not by accident but as the end result of a long historical development that began with the upheavals leading to modern society. The changes are not confined to certain groups and areas of society, but extend into many spheres – from the educational system to the world of work (which could not function without women), from the administration of justice to relations between the sexes (how many of the younger generation of men are willing to be the family's only breadwinner for all their working life?). The new reality cannot be deleted from the world with the stroke of a pen; the way back to women's special role is now barred.

Not only do ever greater numbers of women want to have a job; they must have one for economic reasons (to keep themselves and their children, to buy security in old age and in the event of divorce). In this situation, anyone who onesidedly emphasizes 'family values' in relation to women is bolstering the discrimination against them; it is a model 'conceptually no different from a tax levied on them – "a hidden tax without representation" '.[8]

What is more, the guiding values of freedom and equality associated with this historical development are not an invention of the women's movement; they have their roots in the Enlightenment and the rise of bourgeois society. In the eighteenth and nineteenth centuries, these values applied only to men. But society has moved on since then, old patterns of argument have been crumbling, and the form of 'halfway modernity' has run up against its limits. The demand for freedom and equality reached women too in the course of the twentieth century, and it can no longer be arbitrarily rolled back. It is scarcely conceivable that women will give up the new rights they have won (Giddens 1994a: 13).

Another kind of proposal seeks an institutional solution, on the basis of paid labour, to the tasks traditionally (and to a considerable extent still) performed by women within the family. This would mean, for example, more crèches, more nursery schools and more all-day schools; more assistance for senior citizens, more 'meals on wheels', more nursing homes; more jobs in social work, nursing and care for the elderly.

Such a boost for support services would undoubtedly bring major relief to families, not least to women. But it also poses the question of who would pay for it? The argument has been raging for years and will continue to rage over the costs of long-term care and nursery places. Moreover, as we have seen, the ideal of selfless service that used to be a secret resource in the caring professions has been crumbling as a result of changes in the normal female biography. Since nursing work, despite its considerable physical and mental demands, is also relatively badly paid, there is now a major shortage of skilled staff that will certainly grow worse in the future (*Zwischenbericht* 1994: 587–8; Rabe-Kleberg 1993).

So what does that leave? When the new women's movement began, it raised the revolutionary demand for a redistribution of family labour between the sexes. Three decades later, men do take on more work than they used to – but the change has remained slight. It is still women who bear the brunt of it.

It may be that support is on its way from quite a different quarter. Anyone who follows the German discussion on demographic change or the future of the family (and there are many commissions and conferences on the issues) can see that one theme runs through all the statements, reports and findings: namely, the gaps in provision for children and the elderly. These are becoming the object of academic analysis and, above all, public concern about the future of our society. Authors or groups who can hardly be suspected of belonging to the radical wing of the women's movement are essentially calling for men to play a greater part in care for children and the elderly. Their diction may be more restrained and their style a little convoluted, but there is no mistaking their message. The sociologist Franz-Xaver Kaufmann, for example, writing not in a feminist pamphlet but in a series published by the Federal Chancellor's Office, recognizes that assistance across the generations has hitherto been 'almost exclusively a female domain', but that these conventional forms are today on the decline. Kaufmann sees but one practicable alternative for the future: 'Only if men ... are involved to a greater extent in the production of family welfare is there a hope that the growing doubts among women and the associated questioning of family culture will give way to a new stabilization of the family' (1995: 193).

Much the same analysis, though rather abstractly pitched, is present in a recent German government report on the family: 'Since the tasks performed in the family differ greatly according to gender, age and lifestyle, asymmetries develop between those who perform such services and those who mainly use them' (BMFS 1994: 104). This leads on to a demand for policies to change the future shape of things: 'If unjustified asymmetries in the lives of the two sexes are to be reduced and the family's potential for care of the aged is to be increased, there is no alternative to a policy of care for the elderly in the family on the basis of a changed gender balance of tasks' (1994: 194).

Similar in direction but less laboured in tone is the interim report of the Commission on Demographic Change. This clearly formulates what is required for the future: 'A society that wishes to promote solidarity across the generations no longer has any choice but to concern itself with solidarity between the sexes. In future, stronger action will be necessary to give men more opportunities to carry out tasks in the family, including in "older families".' Here it is explicitly of men that changes are required.

> There seem grounds for concern ... that the impetus in changing gender roles will come only from women and that men will find it considerably harder to change their job-oriented behaviour or even less want to do so. The compatibility of a job with tasks in the family will in future ... have to be strengthened by greater willingness on the part of men to involve themselves in such tasks. (*Zwischenbericht* 1994: 145–6)

A short time ago, former German president Roman Herzog took up such demands and explicitly underlined the responsibilities of men. 'Within the family,' he said, 'it should be made clear how responsibility for the care and upbringing of children can be made consistent ... with job opportunities and plans. This poses questions especially for men, who so far have been only too happy to accept that the resulting conflicts should be resolved by women alone.'[9]

More family work for men – what was a revolutionary demand just a couple of decades ago is today, at the beginning of the twenty-first century, the official refrain and the publicly legitimated model. How things will look in practice is another question. Right now only one thing is certain: future relations between the generations will mainly depend upon whether such ideas are confined to the lip-service oratory of symbolic politics, or whether something serious comes out of them. The next step must be to consider what specific measures need to be introduced (such as care leave and a flexible adjustment of working lives to periods in the family cycle, to take just one well-known example). But if the practical policies fail to materialize, if, despite all the talk, nothing moves in the division of labour between men and women and in care for children and the elderly, then it is anyone's guess what will be the future basis for relations across the generations. To put it plainly, the future contract between the generations will depend on the success of a new contract between the sexes.

5

We Want a Special Child

'*Three thousand deep-frozen embryos destroyed in Great Britain.*'
'*Italian reproductive specialist helps 60-year-old woman to have a child.*' '*American woman pregnant with her own grandchild.*' The new methods of reproductive medicine are still hitting the headlines, but by now they have become widely accepted. They are even, as researchers, doctors and couples constantly inform us, nothing other than medically supported assistance for the most natural thing in the world: the wish for a child of one's own. Only now and again, when some spectacular case becomes known, does the public remember that the new scope for intervention is also throwing up new dilemmas and conflicts. Then, after a few days or weeks of discussion, the excitement subsides again – until the next headline.

What could be more natural than the wish for a child, for a healthy child of one's own? That anyway is what we often think. And yet, as witnesses of the rapid growth in medical technology, we can clearly observe how the ideas, hopes and desires surrounding parenthood are in the process of far-reaching change. Many allusions to this are to be found in the recent literature on prenatal diagnosis and reproductive medicine, where writers again and again report raised expectations and demands among female and male patients. 'Prenatal diagnosis', says geneticist Jan Murken, 'can no longer be removed from the world; but this continuum that runs from really

dangerous illnesses – where everyone can see the unreasonable-
ness of continuing with the pregnancy – through to trivial
demands such as gender selection makes it difficult to draw
the limits. ... I never thought it would suddenly take off like
this and become so widespread' (in Nippert and Horst 1994:
11–12). Similarly for Herman Hepp, director of the women's
department at the Grosshadern Clinic in Munich: 'With these
medical advances [prenatal diagnosis], further desires will be
aroused and deepened. The increasing demand for a healthy
child may in the end go so far that it becomes a kind of "duty to
have a non-handicapped child"' (1994: 267). According to
current thinking, such demands are a product of gross parental
egoism, an expression of their personal inclinations, compulsions or neuroses. But against this view I would like to demonstrate that the desires in question are the continuation of an
epochal trend, namely, the changing form of parenthood in
modernity. To anticipate, the basic thesis will be that the
parents' new duty is to give their child 'the best start in life' –
and that what seems like an over-demanding attitude on their
part is largely an attempt to fulfil this injunction.

In developing this thesis, I will proceed in two stages: first a
brief look back at the social history of parenthood; then a
discussion of present developments in reproductive medicine
and prenatal diagnosis. The argument will be that modern
parenthood has become ever more the object of private planning and decision, public care and responsibility; that what
appears as a natural category has been increasingly opened up
to conscious intervention, thereby acquiring a new dynamic and
leading into new lifestyles; and that all these changes, options
and interventions have together shaped a new relationship between people living today and their descendants.

Parenthood in modernity: the precept of optimum support

We know from various historical studies that for a long time
there was no bringing up of children in the true sense of the

term – that is, with a deliberate awareness of their age and personal development. Instead parents were supposed to ensure that children received moral instruction and were inculcated with a fear of God, obedience and work, as well as providing them with the elementary needs of food and clothing. There was also a certain degree of supervision, to guard against accidents such as drowning, and a lot of physical correction, often in the form of beating.

Only with the transition to modern society did the 'discovery of childhood' (Philippe Ariès), and thus a new era in the history of parenthood, truly begin. The essence of this new attitude was that parents could contribute through proper care and education to the healthy development of their children, and even lay the basis for the whole of their future destiny. One important driving force was the Enlightenment principle, as expressed by Kant: 'Man can become something only through education. He is nothing other than what education makes of him.' The more this acquired the force of a cultural model, the more the tasks of education increased. The child's linguistic and intellectual development, morality and spiritual salvation, all became duties requiring more work from the parents. 'The whole claim of Enlightenment philosophy, with its respect for man as a subject of inalienable rights and its determination to regard each individual as capable of autonomous thought and decision, was now also bestowed upon children, at least prospectively. It became a *duty of parents* to invest such rights in the child' (Flitner 1982: 21; emphasis in the original).

A look at the history of the eighteenth and nineteenth centuries shows that this new interest in education was also being promoted by a far-reaching change in the social structure. For this was the epoch when a phased transition took place from traditional corporatist society to an industrial society regulated by the laws of the market. As people's social position became more open to change, education acquired ever greater importance as the means of supplying skills and knowledge. First of all in the bourgeoisie (and only later in broader sections of the population), efforts were concentrated on the training and development of children in order to claim and secure the greatest possible upward mobility.

In a further extension of parental duties, the question of health came to the fore in the course of the nineteenth century, driven by advances in medicine and in the understanding of the causes of childhood disorders and high infant mortality. Rules for hygiene and nutrition were given special attention, and once again it was the women of the upper middle classes who took to them most readily. Then, in the second half of the nineteenth century, a huge campaign got under way to educate broader sections of women, particularly in the cities. A 'process of civilizing working-class families in matters of hygiene' (Frevert 1985: 421) extended from general principles of health through rules of nutrition to the encouragement of breast-feeding.

This drive, which began with the onset of modernity, gained further momentum in subsequent periods (Beck-Gernsheim 1989: 109ff), especially in the second half of the twentieth century. Again it was advances in medicine, psychology and pedagogy that made it increasingly possible to shape children's lives: physical disabilities, for example, which had to be endured as a given fate earlier in the century, became more and more open to treatment and correction; while new directions in psychological research laid greater stress than before upon the early years of life and blamed lost opportunities of development upon a lack of support. At the same time, a marked rise in average incomes made more widely available childrearing opportunities that had formerly been reserved for a tiny social layer. Birth-rates declined, so that in more and more families only one or two children concentrated all the parents' hopes, ambitions and investments for the future; offspring became a 'scarce resource', whose success was to be actively secured. At a political level, the promotion of education reached out to hitherto disadvantaged groups, and public health was fostered through publicity campaigns and networks of children's doctors, advice centres and evening classes. At many levels parents found themselves under a kind of 'care siege' (Frevert 1985: 421).

As a result of these and similar conditions, the cultural pressure on parents has grown more intense. Less and less can the child be taken as it is, with its physical or mental characteristics and perhaps defects; it has to be the object of all kinds of efforts. As far as possible, all defects are to be corrected (no more squinting, stammering or bed-wetting), all aptitudes to be strengthened (a booming demand for piano lessons, language holidays, summer tennis and winter ski courses). Endless advice on bringing up children appears on the book and magazine market, varying greatly in details but always with the same basic message that the child's development is a private task and personal responsibility of the parents/the mother. On all sides, parents are enjoined to do everything to give their child 'the best start in life'.

In advanced industrial society, then, the physical care of children has in many respects become easier, thanks to the introduction of technology into the home and the availability of such products as disposable nappies or convenience babyfood. But, on the other hand, the modern discovery of childhood has brought with it new aspects and tasks which place growing demands upon parents. As one large-scale study of the family concluded, 'the norm of the ethical and social responsibility of parents' is reaching 'a historically unprecedented level' (Kaufmann et al. 1984: 10).

The supply of prenatal and genetic diagnosis

Until recently the history of parenthood was the history of the ever wider compass of pedagogical instruction. But now a new dynamic has been added to this as reproductive medicine and prenatal testing have enlarged the scope for intervention. The main developments have been: the perfecting of artificial fertilization through freezing techniques and semen banks; *in vitro* fertilization through embryo transfer; the decoding of the genome and the new techniques of prenatal diagnosis based upon it.

With these developments in medicine, biology and genetics, a deliberate 'construction' of parenthood has become more and more of a possibility. This can be used for various purposes, the best known being to help childless couples who want to have a child. Less widely discussed in public is the use of medical technology to fulfil the modern injunction of giving the child the best possible start in life – not only after it is born, but also through prenatal intervention in the biological repertoire.

A new responsibility

In order to highlight the direction of the trend, we shall first consider the sphere of prenatal and genetic diagnoses, where the possibilities have increased most rapidly and the concept of parental responsibility has been changing in the same degree.

First a couple of examples. A pregnant woman: 'I felt caught in a horrible dilemma. All the time I was asked: Have you had the test done? You really should, now that it's possible. ... But what if you have a handicapped child? You've already got two children. You must think of them, and of your husband!' (interview, Schindele 1990: 64). A gynaecologist to a thirty-five-year-old patient: 'A woman – at your age – it's essential. From thirty-five on, you *must* do it' (interview, Schindele 1990: 64). A popular book about the advantages and risks of prenatal diagnostics: 'You should read this book without fail if you ... are responsible about your pregnancy and want to take well-founded decisions' (Blatt 1991: 16–17). With this information 'the responsibility is put where it belongs: with you!' (1991: 25).

What is expressed here is an insidious change in the meaning of responsibility. The more that safe methods of contraception become available, the more widespread becomes the idea of responsible parenthood. Once this referred to the quantitative aspect: only as many children as you can properly bring up and provide for (Häussler 1983: 58–73). Now, with the new possibilities in reproductive medicine and prenatal diagnosis, the concept of responsibility has been moving in the direction of a qualitative choice that begins before birth or perhaps even before conception. The actual formulations, borrowed from the language of government administration, do not directly spell out the aim but speak of 'prevention' (W. Schmid 1988: 77) or 'prophylactic measures'.[1] Such terms have a positive connotation in our society. They sound modern, rational, hygienic, as much part of publicly promoted health care as is the regular brushing of one's teeth. They refer to goals that receive wide support, serving the interests of the individual (preservation of health, avoidance of pain) as well as the interests of society (cost-saving).

More is at stake here, however, than oral hygiene. In plain language, it is a question of avoiding the birth of a handicapped child, either by renouncing biological parenthood altogether or (more likely) by way of a 'tentative pregnancy' and an induced abortion in the event of a genetic deficiency (Rothman 1988). In one information bulletin for doctors, we can read: 'Prenatal genetic diagnosis fundamentally assists the birth of healthy children' – a goal that is assured of general approval, although the formulation is, of course, imprecise at one crucial point. For only in a further clause is it explained how that promise of healthy children is to be fulfilled: 'in so far as children with serious physical or mental disturbances are detected at an early stage, a termination of the pregnancy is thereby made possible.'[2] Such decisions collide with the conventional concept of parental love and recall the dark days of eugenics: in short, they touch on taboos and are therefore often associated with strategies of silence, euphemism or avoidance of the subject. It is no accident that formulations are often used which refer only indirectly to what is at stake. But tendencies are already in the air to praise such behaviour as the expression of a new responsibility, which protects children from a 'grim fate'.[3] Ideas like those of the German philosopher Martin Sass are already gaining ground. High-risk reproductive decisions are, in his view, 'irresponsible towards the society that receives severely handicapped children into its midst' (quoted in BMFT 1984: 123). And in everyday life we can also see a change of attitudes creeping in. Increasingly, women who do not undergo prenatal testing are seen as selfish, ignorant or stupid: 'They prefer to stick their head in the sand rather than to learn the truth' (interview in Schindele 1990: 66). What is evident here is that, as the possibilities for testing become more widespread, the concept of responsibility is filled with a new meaning and insidiously adapted to what is technically feasible. Those who do not play ball appear as irresponsible, suspect, if not downright guilty.

A new guilt

It is not hard to see the logic behind these trends. Responsibility, like health, is a primary value, a lodestar on the horizon of modernity based on the philosophy of the Enlightenment. Responsibility is presented as meaning greater autonomy, much as Kant once defined enlightenment as the 'emergence from self-inflicted immaturity'. Already in that formulation, however, there was a double meaning that pointed to a reverse side: anyone who did not take responsibility counted as irresponsible; any dereliction counted as 'guilt'. Not by chance does the phrase 'reminding someone of their responsibilities' have a threatening undertone. It is precisely this which we can now observe in the field of prenatal diagnosis. On the one hand, in the medical profession as well as in political boards and committees, freedom of choice is declared a basic right and any compulsion on people to undergo tests is constantly forsworn. Everyone must be free to act as they see fit. But on the other hand, in the slipstream of technological advances, a number of small and at first barely noticeable steps attach new meaning to the concept of responsibility, applying ever greater pressure on women to carry out every available test (Hennen et al. 1996: 90–1).

The responsibility at issue has many addressees and reference points. First, as we have just seen, there is the responsibility to society. Then, as quoted above, there is the responsibility to one's family, husband and other children (perhaps even to grandparents hoping for a healthy, cuddly and presentable grandchild). Nor should we forget the responsibility to the unborn child; should it really be burdened with the life of suffering, rejection and dependence that is the fate of the handicapped? Already we hear that, in the event of a genetic defect, the decision to terminate the pregnancy is an act that shows 'caring for the unborn child',[4] or even that it is done for the child's 'benefit'.[5] And women who take up the offer of prenatal testing say that one of their main motives is sympathy for the child that might be handicapped. Such a 'painful existence' should be spared it: 'otherwise it's really a torture for the child' (Hennen et al. 1996: 116 ff). Does care for the child therefore mean today that it is better not to let it see the light of day in the event of a genetic anomaly? Better no life at all than one that begins with the burden of a 'faulty' gene? Abortion out of love for the child?

So many levels of responsibility, so many questions. So much fuel for reproach and self-reproach, for social and moral pressure. As we know from similar situations, this pushes people into taking the tests on offer, 'so we won't have to blame ourselves later on' (Kentenich et al. 1987: 364–70; Parsons and Bradley 1994: 106; Fuchs et al. 1994: 30–1, 148). Figures are now available for prenatal testing: of women whose age put them in a risk group, a good half were opting a few years ago for prenatal diagnosis. And the latest estimates show that the rate has considerably increased since then (Hennen et al. 1996: 78; Bradish et al. 1993: 68–9).[6]

Different countries, different values

It may be revealing in this context to take at look at other cultures and countries. Prenatal diagnosis may, as everyone knows, be used to discover the foetus's sex at an early stage and thus to 'avoid' having a child who is not of the desired gender. This does happen in countries such as India, China or Korea, where a test result indicating a girl leads in many cases to termination of the pregnancy. We feel this to be a barbaric violation of elementary taboos. But from the perspective of those countries' values and living conditions, it might be argued – and is argued – that such practices express not the lack of a basic sense of responsibility but, on the contrary, an awareness of responsibility on the parents' part. It is a conclusion easily reached from the undeniable fact that girls and women are less esteemed there and exposed to multiple forms of discrimination. For if it is permitted, or even morally commanded, to spare a child the grim fate of being handicapped, why should it not be legitimate to help it avoid the perhaps no less grim fate of belonging to the wrong gender?

Many would object that this is a story from strange and distant lands, an exotic special case. Yet, in the age of globalization and worldwide migrations, people from different cultures and countries are no longer only there but also in increasing numbers over here. This leads to an encounter – and not infrequently a clash – between the different values and desires, which doctors active in prenatal diagnosis and reproductive medicine are not the last to experience. Take, for example, the report given by a human geneticist in 1989, to the annual congress of the Human Genetics Society in Munich, concerning a Turkish married couple who wanted a prenatal diagnosis so that, if the embryo was female, they could have the pregnancy terminated. The geneticist pointed out that he himself was completely opposed to eugenics and gender selection, but that the case had been special because the couple, who already had six daughters, were getting on in life and intended to return to Turkey in a few years' time. As their pension would then cover only their living expenses, they would not be able to find the price of a trousseau for another daughter, and without a trousseau the extra girl would have no marriage chances and be excluded from the life that her society considered normal for women. In short, the geneticist concluded, it was a question of another country's customs and values, which we cannot judge according to our own standards.

Now, this kind of gender selection has since been banned in Germany under the Embryo Protection Act, but it is a common view in some nearby Western countries that individual freedom of choice should be respected in such matters and external constraints rejected. The American James Watson, for example, who won the Nobel Prize for his research on the structure of the hereditary molecule, had the following to say:

> I am of the view that only 'unhealthy' offspring should be prevented with the help of prenatal diagnosis. But this is naturally an arbitrary restriction. What is unhealthy? Dyslexia? The king of Sweden is dyslexic, and I am convinced that he would be pleased if this disorder could be prevented in future generations.... Or if a woman has borne seven sons and establishes through prenatal diagnosis that the eighth will be a daughter, then it is an understandable step. These are individual decisions. Everyone should be allowed to make them freely.[7]

Here Watson neatly skirts the key issue, for prenatal diagnosis cannot in fact establish that the child is of the desired sex; all it can do is establish the actual sex of the child, so that, if this is unfavourable, the pregnancy can be terminated. Watson's example is untypical – to put it mildly – given that in the overwhelming majority of cases it is a boy rather than a girl that is desired. But his message certainly comes over clearly: namely, that gender selection is understandable under certain circumstances.

And if it is understandable to avoid children of the wrong sex, how about children with the wrong skin colour? Here again it may be argued that, under certain circumstances, a corresponding selection may be humanly understandable, perhaps even morally compelling. In view of the well-known horrors of German history, no one would say this here in public. But such taboos do not apply in most other countries, where it is possible to speak and write in a much less 'charged' manner. In a British article on the ethics of genome analysis, for example, we read:

> In a society where discrimination exists, certain attributes are, without doubt, considered to be highly desirable and an individual lacking such attributes can expect to be disadvantaged, to a greater or lesser degree. Thus, it can be argued that not all forms of eugenics are necessarily undesirable. Selection of embryos or foetuses that possess certain characters might be ethically justi-

fied on the grounds of desire for the future welfare of the child. There is, for example, clear justification for selection based upon … skin colour in a society where discrimination adversely affects equality of opportunity. (Wood-Harper and Harris 1996: 282)

From such examples we can see how the formula 'in the child's best interests' offers scope for many different evaluations and interpretations. And we can also see how much that which appears morally questionable or reprehensible in Germany today is seen and practised quite differently elsewhere – where it may count as normal, humanly understandable, or even morally compelling.

The promises of reproductive medicine

In recent years, a wide range of more or less intricate procedures have been developed in reproductive medicine to offer help to those who are childless but would like to have children. The best known of such groups are couples who suffer from some biological impediment, but there are also newer groups, less present in the public mind, who have increasingly appeared with the pluralization of lifestyles and for various reasons demand medical assistance to fulfil their wish for a child. There are women and men who once got sterilized and now regret the decision (for example, in the context of a new relationship); women who are already past the menopause but hope to become mothers through an egg donor; gay and lesbian couples who wish to become parents; and single persons who, though without a partner, do not wish to be left without a child.

However different these motives may be, they all point towards the 'technically assisted reproduction' which is covertly, as it were, clearing the way for new forms of parenthood. For, in the wake of technological changes and the new opportunities they raise, the wish to have a child may be associated with a wish to influence its nature and constitution. What applies in the realm of prenatal diagnosis is even more clearly observable in reproductive medicine: many prospective parents see medical technology as a service and, as doctors often complain, develop marked symptoms of 'consumerist behaviour' (Hepp 1994: 267). A child is no longer enough, no, it must be a special child; a new kind of 'child planning mentality' is on the rise (Daele 1986: 157–8). All this is not an accident, nor a mere expression of parental egoism. It is already programmed in the procedures themselves, as reproductive medicine makes new choices possible and often even necessary.

Ideal solutions and choices

A good illustration of this is the wish to have a child with the help of a sperm or egg donor or a surrogate mother. In the United States it is common practice to show interested parties a catalogue of fine and healthy donors or surrogates, listed according to their relevant attributes. The clients can, indeed must, then choose someone from the list. And if there is a choice, why not select the best one on offer? Which shopper, when asked to choose between various items, would consciously take one that he or she finds less appealing? Similarly here, since a choice must anyway be made, the obvious course is to make it fit one's own ideal picture, to will the roulette ball to land on certain properties. Some 'customers' therefore bet on intelligence, others on good health, still others on blue eyes or sporting performance. The wishes are not distributed at random, but follow the same trend to optimization that we have identified before. As a report on the largest US sperm bank puts it, the selected donor is supposed 'to look as much like the husband as possible, "only please without the big nose"', or some other defect; he should have 'the best of the spouse, mixed with some corrections from the donor'. Single women, for their part, often send photos of film stars to indicate their ideal donor, and hence their ideal future child (Biel 1995: 32).

Similar tendencies have been reported from the realm of *in vitro* (that is, test-tube) fertilization, which not so long ago still made the headlines and aroused intense public debate, but which now is almost a routine treatment for sterility. According to doctors working in this field, patients not infrequently present their wish for a child with a demanding and insistent attitude – in one case, as if they were purchasing a product 'by the colour of its hair and eyes' (Fuchs et al. 1994: 32). Jacques Testart, one of the scientists behind France's first test-tube baby, is even more caustic: 'My dear parents, IVF is happy to think that it will soon be able to offer you egg cells à la carte; the lab undertakes to guarantee your chosen gender and standards. When a touch more progress is made, you will be able to choose from a range as in a pet shop: hair colour, leg length, ear shape and certificate of good health' (1988: 22). Testart's experience tells him that IVF will soon also be used for gender selection and genetic correction: 'Don't think you will be able to stop parents from personally choosing the egg once that becomes possible' (1988: 25).

> In my view, the birth of a child whose gender is not the one desired by the parents will also be the cause of pain, no less than the pain couples feel today when their desire for children goes unfulfilled. Psychiatrists will rightly point to the dangers for the couple's mental equilibrium and the child's own development if the technical assistance on offer is refused. (1988: 115)

What was then presented as a vision of the future has since become reality. One British reproductive specialist, for example, openly offers IVF for gender selection (only he does it in Italy and Saudi Arabia, as this is prohibited in Britain). There are certainly many takers, and he has a calm retort to any objection: 'The practice of medicine always involves... intervening in nature. Heart transplants or gender selection: where's the difference?'[8] As to IVF selection according to skin colour, a few years ago a black woman had egg cells implanted from a white woman, specifically in order to improve the eventual child's chances in life. The *Economist* commented: 'If one is to see a wickedness here, it is not that of a mother who wants the best for her child, but that of a society which judges children by colour and metes out opportunities accordingly.'[9]

If the hoped-for pregnancy is achieved, the tendency towards offspring optimization continues with attempts to prevent the whims and accidents of nature. It is reported from German IVF centres, for example, that women who become pregnant with the help of newly available technologies often also have recourse to prenatal diagnosis (Fuchs et al. 1994: 156), in spite of the fact that it involves the risk of causing a miscarriage. However intense and compelling is the desire to have a child, the desire that the child should be free of defects is still more intense and compelling.

Product liability

Not just any child; it must be as free of 'defects' as possible. This demand is still more apparent when we come to 'children made to order' – that is, through clinics which offer the services (how else is one to call them?) of sperm or egg donors and surrogate mothers. The selection processes, at least at the better clinics, are designed to meet the parents' expectation by checking the medical history of prospective donors and testing them for infections – in short, by applying stringent safety standards.[10] In the United States, surrogate mother contracts usually contain a clause requiring prenatal testing if pregnancy actually occurs, and an undertaking to abort in the event of a genetic abnormality (see e.g. Field 1988: 65–7).

But what if the eventual baby does not correspond to the parents' wishes, if in spite of everything it presents some handicap or chronic affliction? Then (at least under US law) a legal dispute may ensue. One couple in California, for example, sued a sperm bank for damages because their daughter was found to have an incurable hereditary disorder. She had been conceived with test-tube sperm, even though the donor in question had previously informed the sperm bank company that one of his aunts suffered from a brain disease, and, as it later transpired, several of his relatives had polycystic brains or had already died because of them. The trial is now supposed to establish the extent of the company's liability for its products.[11]

We Want a Special Child

As we have seen, there is a widespread view that wishes of this kind testify to personal inclinations and neuroses on the part of the parents – from control freakery to manic perfectionism. In my view, however, this falls short of the mark. For it overlooks the fact that such behaviour meshes perfectly with a historical trend which attributes ever more tasks and duties to parents; and that the uses of high-tech medical products actually reflect a further extension of this trend into areas previously closed to human intervention. 'Optimization of the child's life chances' here becomes a tendency to 'genetic optimization of the child', and this has a powerful logic of its own. In a society where health, performance and fitness are of prime importance, and where they are no longer a natural destiny but a task and responsibility for human action, the responsibility applies also to parents before the birth or even the conception of their child.

The side-effects of optimization

It is another question, of course, whether all the methods of optimization and selection provided by medical technology actually serve the child's well-being and are conducive to the rights and interests of others. If we try to arrange for our children's biological make-up to have the fewest possible defects, how is this likely to change our handling of them? How do we react if they do not turn out as in our ideal picture, if all the optimal planning does not produce optimal results? How are parents-to-be supposed to act 'freely', 'autonomously' and 'responsibly' when they are overwhelmed by the complexity of medical information, the authority of doctors' knowledge and the anonymity of modern technology? How are they to cope with the bewildering new options and all the dilemmas, forced choices and conflicts bound up with them? How will society itself change if the handling of health, illness and disability is organized down to the last detail on an ever more technological basis? What will become of mutual support if the 'avoidance' of weakness, deviation and abnormality becomes the supreme practical maxim? Is the defect-free society ultimately a society that has turned its back on solidarity?

101

All these are questions that have been heatedly debated since the rapid development of biotechnology. The new possibilities are a subject of discussion, and the so-called 'side-effects' of technology have become an increasing concern among scientists and politicians, the media and the general public. The search is on for rules to counteract the unbridled spread of the new methods and procedures, to direct their application into paths agreed by society, and to recognize the possible conflicts of interest among various social groups, so that, if necessary, the rights of the weakest sections can be protected. The extent to which the 'genetic optimization' of offspring is able to assert itself will depend not least upon the outcome of this public weighing of risks and side-effects.

What future?

Many of the new medical technologies described in this chapter are already practised on a daily basis in Germany; others are not permitted here but are used on a wide scale in other countries. Many of the examples sound familiar; others may appear remote or even exotic. In each case, however, we can see that they are more and more opening up the possibility of a deliberate 'construction' of parenthood. The first signs of 'programmed heredity' (Bräutigam and Mettler 1985) are beginning to appear, and 'made-to-measure humans' (Daele 1985) enter visions of the possible future:

> Modern biology turns attributes of human nature that used to define the reference limits for technology into spheres of operation for technology itself. ... Under the impact of science and technology, human nature itself is becoming contingent: that is, it may also be different from how it is at present. It thus opens itself up for decision, and actually requires decisions to be made. Even to refrain from any intervention then appears as one more conscious act in the production of human nature. (1985: 11ff)

102

In the modern world, then, parenthood is less than ever a natural condition; it is hedged round with theories and experts and opened up through new technological options. Parenthood is becoming more and more a planning project, an object of constant effort and optimization, while the unborn child above all is subjected to all manner of 'preliminary investigations'. In Theresa Marteau's words: 'Before the development of prenatal testing... the fetus was assumed to be healthy, unless there was evidence to the contrary. The presence of prenatal testing and monitoring shifts the balance toward having to prove the health or abnormality of the fetus' (quoted in Boston 1994: 119). No one can say for sure whether all the technical possibilities of today and tomorrow will be employed, whether the trend to genetic optimization of offspring will one day break all bounds or be held back under various constraints. Other factors in play, apart from the technological developments themselves, are legal regulations, political incentives or sanctions, economic conditions and cultural models. But there is a lot to suggest that a new form of human control will 'change the concept of parenthood, so that parental responsibility for the newly emerging life will widen in accordance with the new technological possibilities' (Hoffmann-Riem 1988: 40). If this prognosis is correct, the parents of the future will indeed be faced with quite novel questions, actions and pressures to decide.

6

Towards the Multicultural Family

A problem of social order

In the theatres of New York one rarely sees any blacks; there are few roles for blacks and few black playwrights. One exception is the dramatist August Wilson, himself the light-skinned son of a black woman and a German-American baker. In a recent speech, he fulminated against the power relations in the country's culture and provocatively concluded that in a white-dominated society blacks need a theatre of their own. This sparked off a major public controversy, in which one woman pointedly asked: 'I am half Balinese, half Irish. My grandmother comes from the Philippines and my grandfather from Poland. I grew up in Texas and now live in New York. What kind of a theatre do you propose for me?'[1]

This is in several ways a symptomatic story. For over the last few decades, and especially the last few years, the number of binational/bicultural marriages has risen quite considerably in the United States, as it has in Germany and other countries. In other words, there are more and more couples whose two partners are markedly different in origin, whether in respect of nationality, cultural group, religion or skin colour. Through such couples – and even more through their children, of course – there has been an increase in the number of people who cannot fit themselves or be fitted by officialdom into the conventional categories ('black', 'Italian', 'Jewish'), because they are not any one of these, or rather because they are several at once. How, for example, should Jews with Italian grand-mothers be classified?

In the past, too, some people fell between the categories, though there were fewer of them. But today there is not only quantitative growth but also a new qualitative aspect. Whereas children from such families often used to have only one option open to them – that is, they belonged exclusively to one side of the family, renouncing, forgetting and sometimes actually hushing up the other side – a clear change in consciousness has taken place in recent years. From the United States, the country so fond of seeing itself rightly or wrongly as a 'melting pot', it is reported that more and more people no longer want to tie themselves down to one or the other side of the family (Spickard 1989 *passim*; Rosenblatt et al. 1995: 142, 203ff; Tizard and Phoenix 1995: 3–4, 46ff), and similar trends are discernible in Germany and elsewhere (Oguntoye et al. 1992). Rather than anxiously adapting, they consciously lay claim to an identity that is both at once, not one at the price of the other's exclusion. They conceive their identity as bicultural or even multicultural; they see themselves as 'black Jews', 'Japanese Americans' or even 'Afro-Germans'. The motto here is: 'I don't have to choose, I'm both' (Teo 1994); or, even more bluntly, 'I'm neither black nor white, I'm multi-coloured.'[2]

Such trends towards binational/bicultural marriage and identity are not just a matter of private decision; they are also a politically explosive issue. For one of the features of the modern state is that individuals are constantly required to clas-sify themselves by nationality or ethnic origin, giving simple answers that various institutions can process and use to allocate rights, duties or claims (whether for military service, work permits or residence rights). The legal distinction between members and non-members is thus not a neutral one but serves to include and to exclude individuals in relation to the resources of society. Or, as Jürgen Habermas puts it, membership status within a country forms 'the basis for the allocation of positions under the law which together make up citizenship status' (1992: 151–2).

In this light, it is obvious that those who burst open national or cultural classifications constitute by their mere existence a problem of social order. They are the disruptive factor in the social mechanism, because they cannot be represented within the usual clear-cut categories; they are often quite literally 'misfits'. Their existence (for the state as for the ordinary citizen) is shifting and ambivalent, not to say dubious or suspect. This inevitably raises the question of the social, political and legal position of those who do not fit into the conventional categories of unambiguous ascription. How should society proceed with them? How do they wish to be regarded, how do others wish to regard them, how is their identity to be conceived? Should they be able to define their own identity, or does society have the right to decide? What rules of classification are possible or practicable or politically desirable? What conflicts might arise if one or the other interpretation is chosen, and how would they then be resolved?

The topicality and political explosiveness of these basic issues may be seen in, among other things, the debate on dual citizenship. Various societies have tried in a number of ways to come up with answers, and I would like to consider two from the spectrum of possibilities. First, society may attempt – through a state decree or administrative decision – to classify within a clear-cut category those whose origin or family structure does not admit of such precise allocation. Or, second, society may try to devise new categories that signal the in-between status of such groups, perhaps by meticulously sorting and distinguishing them in further ways. As we shall see, there are historical examples of these different courses, both of which may be theoretically understood as social constructions which, for obvious reasons (their attempt to force unruly reality into existing schemas), produce their own paradoxes, contradictions and absurdities, with sometimes comical, sometimes horrifying, consequences for those affected by them.

I should now like to take you, the reader, on a surprising and at first perhaps irritating journey. Let us begin by looking at two constellations from the past, each of which in its way will then lead us up towards the present. Why this kind of route? The reason is that, from the wealth of stories and personal fates, a picture will gradually take shape showing the many layers of the multicultural family, its biographical, social and political dimensions at various points in time (and, hardly less important, the blind spots and errors and the confusions of different eras). By taking this path, we shall also come to see how time and again the traces of yesterday extend into the present.

The example of the United States: who is a black?[3]

In many states of the USA, marriage between blacks and whites was for a long time not only frowned upon but legally prohibited, yet over the centuries there were always some cross-colour alliances from which a number of children issued. As the historian Paul Spickard has shown, a small number of mixed marriages even occurred in the era of slavery, although much more common were various forms of concubinage and forced sexual intercourse (for example, between plantation owners and female slaves). The pattern of sexual relations was thus largely shaped by the power hierarchy prevailing between blacks and whites (1989: 235–6).

Because of this history there are a considerable number of individuals, especially among blacks but also among whites, who have ancestors of the 'other' skin colour. So long as open discrimination still existed, the question of how society should treat such people was constantly present at many levels of daily life (and even today subtler variants are far from having disappeared). How should this group of people be classified legally and socially? How should the surrounding world react to them? Which schools should they attend, which hotels and restaurants should they be able to frequent, which clubs should they be allowed to join? And, last but not least, whom should they be free to marry?

Trying to put some order into things

In the official censuses of the nineteenth and early twentieth centuries, efforts were made to address the basic problem of classification by drawing a number of new distinctions. But the methods used remained crude and arbitrary, at best only touching the surface of the complex sets of circumstances, and the results have to be considered questionable. Spickard has described how random were the processes of ascribing individuals to categories of the population:

> The Bureau of the Census made counts of mulattoes as well as Blacks for 1860, 1870, 1890, 1910, and 1920. But the term *mulatto* was interpreted variously. In 1850 and 1860, census takers received no instructions on how to decide if a person were a mulatto. One assumes the enumerators relied on eyeball estimates of color and features, together with whatever background information they might pick up. In 1870, 1910, and 1920, bureau employees were told to regard 'full-blooded Negroes' as 'black', and 'all Negroes having some proportion of white blood' as 'mulattoes'. In 1890 these vague instructions were briefly replaced by a more precise set of criteria. That year, 'blacks' were 'persons having from three to five eighths Negro blood'; 'quadroons' and 'octoroons' had even less African ancestry. The problem, of course, is that the census takers seldom had sufficient family background data on which to base such fine gradations. As the 1890 census report admitted, 'These figures are of little value.' (Spickard 1989: 433)

The ascription problem must have been even more difficult in daily life, where relations often consisted of fleeting, anonymous contacts. In these conditions, there was certainly no time to study family histories or to draw complex distinctions; it was necessary to take short cuts and to use the simplest rules of thumb. In many areas of society (especially those considered exclusive), a simple and restrictive 'whites only' rule applied during the era of racial discrimination – which meant that only those who were 'completely white' (or at least looked so in appearance) could be admitted as members. Anyone with the least drop of 'black blood' from however distant a past, if it was externally visible or otherwise known, had to stay outside. 'Whites only' meant 'off limits' for them.

But what was to be done if the issue was not a brief encounter but a long, perhaps a lifelong, relationship – a marriage? Since, in the thinking of the time, the public interest was at stake in such matters, the state retained the power to decide on them (indeed, the last laws banning mixed marriage in a state of the USA were lifted only in 1967 (Spickard 1989: 374)). This again raised the question of who was black, or who was to be con-sidered so in uncertain or doubtful cases. Some states devised precise rules and yardsticks to settle the issue, following the symbolic 'one drop' rule, and it is interesting to note the lengths to which various states went to trace that drop and the different definitions they employed. 'Liberal' Oregon went back only as far as the grandparents, so that one black grandfather or grand-mother sufficed to define someone as black. Louisiana and North Carolina, on the other hand, went back two further generations, so that anyone who had one black great-great-grandparent counted as black (1989: 375). It is hardly surpris-ing that, where the hunt delved so deep into the past, the rules could hardly be put into practice and the conclusions often became random or arbitrary.

Confusion, contradictions, paradoxes

The confusion arose not only from the fact that a procedure which measured a person's whole ancestry by a single 'drop of blood' was itself inherently absurd, but also because the hunt often turned up no clearly identifiable traces in the past and left ample scope for fantasy and rumour. Moreover, it is easy to overlook the laws of biology and genetics that play a role in all this. In particular, the principle of random distribution ex-plained by Mendel in his theory of heredity (remember the red, white and pink roses) states that, in a mixed family with both black and white ancestors, the shade of the children's skin colour is often a lottery and even siblings may be quite unlike one another in external appearance.

Now, if skin colour operates as the main criterion for the allocation of life chances yet is partly dependent upon the vagaries of nature, and if, therefore, individuals may often appear to be other than they are officially allocated as being, it seems reasonable to suppose that many of those affected will seek to exploit the loopholes and contradictions in the prevailing system of classification – that is, they will seek to get round its rules of ascription as a way of escaping discrimination. And indeed there have been cases (for obvious reasons we do not know the precise number) where people of mixed ancestry but with a light skin colour have moved away and tried to live as 'whites' in different surroundings. The term 'passing' was coined to denote such behaviour, and even if it occurred very infrequently it gave rise to all manner of fears and fantasies, becoming the stuff of countless novels, films and television series. Henry Louis Gates, Harvard Professor of English and Afro-American Studies and himself from a mixed, mainly 'black' family, has told in his autobiography of the emotions and tearful scenes that such television episodes (which he saw as a child) caused among black viewers (1995: 23–4). And the historian Paul Spickard has described typical situations and forms of 'passing', as well as the price that individuals had to pay for them (1989: 333–6; see also Rogge 1965).

Why new controversies are developing today

With the banning of racial discrimination and the growing consciousness of blacks, such forms of 'passing' to the situation and privileges of whites have become much less common. There have even been cases of passing in the opposite direction, from white to black – or so it is claimed. Thus, in one town in California, it has become a matter of public debate whether what one politician alleges about his rival is in fact true: namely, that he ran for election with false credentials because, although white, he passed himself off as black to gain political advantage.[4]

What here is truth and what is legend? Is it a case of political defamation or of political opportunism? Possibly both sides are correct, in the sense that they base themselves not on actual skin colour but on belonging to the social category of black or white. Although the story sounds a little fishy, it may also be that the 'one drop' rule is here being applied literally – and how often were there not suspicions and accusations of the reverse kind, designed to suggest a (real or invented) black ancestor in order to destroy a white man politically and to discredit him in the eyes of society.

One thing at least is here immediately evident: the attempt to solve the social problem of classification can lead into a maze of error and confusion, pretence and suspicion. This happens because the social ascriptions are anything but value-neutral; they decide people's life chances and, in the case of social outcasts, bring humiliation, exclusion and persecution. It is also apparent that describing a category as 'right' or 'wrong' is also a social construct, because it depends upon the social climate and political conjuncture. Whereas, in the era of slavery, a black skin meant brutal exploitation and subjugation, it might later, in the age of new legal regulations and growing self-assertiveness of minority groups, occasionally bring advantages such as access to certain resources (for example, in education, the labour market or public housing). When this happens – as it has done, at least to some extent, through 'affirmative action' programmes in the United States – the cards in the game of ethnic ascription are reshuffled. One study of ethnic relations in the USA today states that there are now 'political constructions of ethnicity' based only in part or not at all upon ancestry, which develop chiefly out of 'competition over equal life chances' (Neckel 1997). In other words, it is not just a matter of personal preference or neurosis whether someone keeps quiet about their black (or Indian or Jewish) grandmother or consciously reveals and emphasizes it; instead, it depends to a large degree upon political conditions of minority advancement or discrimination – in short, upon positive or negative sanctions associated with ancestors of this or that origin.

111

From the history of National Socialism: who is a Jew?

When the Nazis came to power in Germany in 1933, they immediately started to put into practice what they had announced in advance in their writings, the programme of depriving Jews of their rights, separating them out and subjecting them to persecution (see e.g. Walk 1981; Rosenstrauch 1988). From the ban on keeping domestic animals, using public libraries, sitting on park benches or going to the cinema or theatre, through the official debarment from certain professions or public posts and the confiscation of property, to the final collection, deportation and extermination: this was the range of measures used to expel Jews from the 'German national body' so that the country would become *judenfrei*.

But here too a classification problem presented itself. In the United States, the programme of racial discrimination against blacks could at least refer to the visible criterion of skin colour (even if this gave rise to the contradictory interpretations we have seen). But there was not even this when it came to deciding who was a Jew or not; in Germany the situation right from the start was extremely complicated.

After centuries of restrictions on their freedom, German Jews gained civil rights and citizenship through various acts of emancipation legislated in the course of the nineteenth century. Many kinds of discrimination and prejudice still persisted, to be sure, but by the early twentieth century more and more Jews lived a life which scarcely differed from that of their non-Jewish neighbours.[5] Many families distanced themselves from the Jewish tradition and its customs. Some lived as three-day Jews (as they were ironically called), because they went to the synagogue only on the three main holidays of the Jewish Year; others abandoned the Jewish religious community and went over to Christianity; others practised a kind of symbiosis by observing Jewish holidays as well as celebrating Easter and Christmas; and still others linked up more closely with their non-Jewish surroundings through marriage and the founding of a 'mixed family'. But, regardless of whether they still practised

112

the Jewish religion or belonged only externally to the Jewish religious community or even distanced themselves from it altogether, most of them identified with Germany and saw themselves as completely and self-evidently German. They felt little in common with the Jews from Eastern Europe who, at the beginning of the twentieth century, started to come to Germany in greater numbers only to find themselves cold-shouldered and treated with mistrust. They, the German Jews, were first and foremost Germans and only then Jews as well – a clear sign of this being the very name of their 'Central Association of German Citizens of the Jewish Faith'.

This was the situation which the Nazis found. The problem from their point of view was how to reverse the process of assimilation and to make dissimilar again those who had become so similar. The strategy they adopted was twofold: on the one hand, lavish propaganda exercises represented the Jews as 'alien' and 'other', by constructing a distorted image of them as spongers and parasites off the body of the German nation; on the other hand, the immediate establishment of a special legal status for Jews excluded them and robbed them of their rights.

Grades of separation

But the problem remained of what to do about the considerable number of 'mixed' families with spouses of Jewish and non-Jewish origin, who had grown close to each other through the affection and companionship of everyday life, through marriage and children. As the Nazis saw it, this group was the source of a special danger of 'national poisoning'. It is not surprising, therefore, that the new rulers very soon introduced explicit measures against this section of the population, designed in fact to obliterate it as a group. Pressure was brought to bear upon non-Jewish partners in such marriages to apply for divorce (which some, though not many, did do), but even greater effort was put into the prevention of further alliances of this kind. The Protection of German Blood and Honour Law of 19 September 1935 stipulated:

§ 1 Marriage between Jews and German nationals or others of related blood is forbidden. Marriages concluded in spite of this provision are null.

§ 2 Extramarital intercourse between Jews and German nationals or others of related blood is forbidden.

But what of marriages concluded before this law and still valid? What especially of the children from such marriages? They were a huge obstacle to the stated aim of separating Germans and Jews, and the new rulers soon got to work on it. A complicated system of grades was devised for the methodical bureaucratic definition of who had Jewish ancestry and how much, who was or should be counted as a Jew. A Jew was anyone 'descended from at least three racially full-Jewish grandparents, full-Jewish being anyone who belongs to the Jewish religious community'. This resulted (to name the most important of the newly created categories) in 'recognized Jews', 'religious Jews', 'simple mixed marriages' and 'privileged mixed marriages', 'grade one half-breeds' and 'grade two half-breeds'.

In addition, there was a set of further specifications for membership in one or another category (even including the spouse's state of health and the children's place of residence).[6] But this complicated structure could hardly be applied in everyday situations calling for swift judgement, and external appearance was hardly enough to clear things up, as Jews often did not look as 'Jewish', or non-Jews as 'Aryan' or 'Nordic', as Nazi ideology liked to paint them. For everyday situations, therefore, signs had to be created which made it immediately apparent whether a person belonged to the group of 'others': all men and women who did not have a recognizably 'Jewish' name had to add a stylized Jewish forename to their own forename in all official documents (Walter Mayer thus became Walter 'Israel' Mayer, or Anna Binder became Anna 'Sara' Binder); and a large 'J' was stamped in their passports and ration cards. In order that there should be no misunderstanding even in the most fleeting encounter, Jews (or, more precisely, most of those who counted as Jews under the new system of rules) were obliged to wear a label in a visible and clearly prescribed place: the so-called

Judenstern or 'Star of David'. A decree of 1 September 1941 states:

> From 15/9/1941 Jews who have reached six years of age are forbidden to appear in public without a Star of David.... This does not apply to Jewish spouses living in mixed marriages when offspring of the marriage who are not considered Jews are present, or whose only son has fallen in the war, nor to the Jewish wife in a childless mixed marriage for so long as the marriage lasts.

The labyrinth of 'right' and 'wrong' grandparents[7]

The system of rules just described claimed to be methodical and precise, but in reality it was complex and contradictory in its jumbling together of biological and social criteria. It made reference to descent and supposed 'race', but then defined race by referring to religious affiliation and even brought in the gender, marital status and circumstances of family members, while in everyday life it was often 'appearances' that counted most in the classification of a particular individual.

Such a system was bound to cause confusion, which could in some circumstances be life-threatening and in others life-saving. New scope was created for supposition, gossip and rumour when – partly as a result of some classificatory juggling – the suspicion spread that someone or other was of Jewish descent.[8] Conversely, there were mistakes and oversights in the bureaucratic registration process, as Jewish ancestors were disregarded in individuals from 'mixed' families and the 'Jewish and half-breed card files' were not always complete (see e.g. Braach 1994: 141; Brückner 1980: 122; Hecht 1984: 148). In one case after another from everyday life, someone was classified as belonging to the Nordic race on the basis of external appearance, when in fact he or she had 'other' ancestors. Here are two poignant stories.

> One day a preliminary check was made during the English class. I was very good in this subject and was often picked on to

answer. At the concluding discussion with the teacher, the
official asked [the teacher] who 'that girl is, that prototype of
the Nordic race'. She is the only *half-Jew* in her class, she said
with great delight. (Hecht 1984: 53)

I fell in love with the girl who would later become my first wife.
She had the snow-white, slightly freckled skin of the true red-
head, a tiny little snub nose, and a large, very beautiful mouth
with immaculate teeth. The eighteen-year-old came from Graz
and spoke a dialect very close to my own original one. She wore
Austrian traditional dress, the so-called *dirndl*, which suited her
down to the ground.

Then it turned out that 'she was a full and religious Jew, that
her Styrian origin was not without blemish and her father was
a Jewish immigrant from Eastern Europe' – in short, she was a
'dialect-speaking Jewess who would have cut a perfect figure in
tourist publicity for the "Ostmark" [Austria]'.[9]

Since the Nazis' system of classification was both complicated and potentially life-threatening, it was as if tailor-made to
provoke evasive manoeuvres. Personal reports often speak of
attempts to evade or outwit racist classification criteria, to
touch up 'unsuitable' family connections, to provide 'dangerous' ancestors with a new identity. Some Jews also tried to hide
from the Nazis by 'going underground', or by switching to the
Aryan side of the family and adopting an Aryan identity, in
moves reminiscent of 'passing' from black to white in America.
But the paucity of material suggests that few dared risk this in
Germany, and that the great majority did not elude classification as Jews (with death as the most common result in the
end). This may well seem paradoxical. For if, as we have seen,
Jews were hardly distinguishable in their everyday lives from
their non-Jewish neighbours, 'passing' would have been
relatively easy to achieve. Why did only few venture on this
course?

The first answer which suggests itself is that the registration
authorities were more thorough in Germany than in the United
States, that despite occasional slips and mistakes there were just
too many documents and too few gaps for a change of identity

to be such an easy matter. This seems plausible enough – yet it can only be part of the answer, and then only the external part, as it were. When one considers what used to be known as the age of assimilation, one has good reason to suppose that more deeply rooted obstacles were also involved. Thinking of themselves as Germans first of all, as German 'nationals', many Jews must for a long time have been unable to comprehend that they were to be suddenly excluded from their own land; that the new rulers (and with them a good part of the German people) saw them instead as radically 'other'. The tragic mistake thus lay in the disparity between how they saw themselves and how others saw them. If this interpretation is correct, then the answer to the paradox is to be found in the paradox itself. If most German Jews did not attempt 'passing', it was not because they stood out too much but, on the contrary, because they took their German identity completely for granted.

At the time when 'passing' from black to white used to occur in the United States, racial discrimination was openly and publicly practised and all blacks were aware of what to expect. They knew themselves to be excluded; they knew that they had fewer rights and that their lives had been fenced in with numerous restrictions. Over the generations they had developed a feeling for alarm signals in the everyday world around them. In Germany, by contrast, Jews faced quite a different situation in the early part of the twentieth century. Even if they often encountered prejudice in their daily lives, their basic experience had been the increase in rights that had taken place during the nineteenth century. They, their parents and their grandparents had personally lived through this. It was what gave them a sense of security – a false sense, as it turned out.

The advent of National Socialism shattered this security, and many who survived underwent a deep change in their identity. This is especially striking in some of those for whom Jewishness had meant next to nothing before Hitler came to power, because their families had long since taken their distance from it. According to these survivors, they became Jews through the

Nazis – not through race or biology, nor through religion, but through a shared fate. It was the fate of persecution which, in their view, turned them into Jews.

> Jewish festivals and Jewish religious services did not feature in my childhood – only Christmas, Easter and St Nicholas's Day, with all the trappings that make children happy. We knew from an early age that we were Jews, but despite the religious education it remained a vague concept that was not really part of our lives. When I asked my father about it as a child, he said that it meant nothing to him; all he felt was German. 'How come?' I said ... 'What does it mean then?' He could not explain to me and fended off my questions ... as if they were unimportant to him. ... And was it really easy to answer them? Since then, there has been the bitter minimal definition: 'A Jew is someone who has been defined as Jewish by Hitler.'[10]

> The practice of the Jewish religion did not exist even residually in my parents' home. ... What three generations of assimilation had made of us was a stronger influence than pale and distant origins about which we had only learnt knowledge. ... After the insane slaughter of six million Jews by Hitler, I was only one thing: a Jew. ... What those twelve years which weighed as heavy as a thousand had made of me could no longer be reversed. I no longer *wanted* to reverse it.[11]

How the search for roots looks today

There is yet another irony of history. It may be that today (and this too recalls the United States, as in our story of a white politician claiming to be black) there are new forms of 'passing' in which people of non-Jewish origin take on a Jewish identity. The German ministry of the interior anyway has doubts about the influx of immigrants into the Jewish community in Germany since 1989; the suspicion is that many of them are not really Jews but are passing themselves off as such in order to be given a Russian exit visa and a residence permit in the West.[12] Often precise documentation cannot be obtained, since Jewish community organizations and the practice of the Jewish religion were suppressed in the former Soviet Union. So who can say what is the truth? Who can know who is who? Again we see how, with a change in the political situation, the search for ethnic roots can change direction and many bizarre rules can develop as a result. 'It is macabre. The Germans used to demand proof that someone was not a Jew. Now they want proof that someone is a Jew.'[13]

Difficult concepts: the burden of history

We began this chapter with multicultural families and then looked at two historical attempts to classify who was a black, who was a Jew, who belonged to an intermediate category. This journey through history was important in explaining why it is difficult today to talk at all about the subject. Here no terms are 'objective'; they all carry within them the burden of history, which is also a history of racial exclusion, separation and discrimination. Any discussion of it therefore involves treading very carefully. On the one hand, there are familiar terms (often used even today) that have become problematic because of history; on the other hand, there are new terms artificially coined as a neutral substitute for old ideological associations. In between lies a most delicate balancing act.

Let us begin with an obvious example: the term 'mixed marriage'. This was current in Germany well before Hitler, when it denoted inter-confessional marriages of any kind (Catholic–Evangelical as well as Jewish–Catholic, for example). But in 1935, two years after they came to power, the Nazis decreed that the expression should be used to refer only to marriages between 'Aryans' and 'non-Aryans' (Kleiber and Gömusay 1990: 68) – which is why in people's minds today it is inseparably bound up with Nazi race policy and legislation. Similarly, in the USA a number of terms are in circulation which involve uncertainties and historical burdens of their own. 'Multiracial couple', for instance, is widely used, even though the word 'race' has sinister biological connotations in other contexts in English, as it does even more strongly in German. In order to avoid these, the preference in Germany is to speak of 'multicultural families' – but it is a modern expression which runs into difficulties when applied retrospectively to earlier periods of history.

So what is to be done? Up to this point I have tried to steer round the problem with the help of circumlocutions and auxiliary words, both sneaking in the term 'mixed families', for example, and at the same time (note the inverted commas) endeavouring to keep a discreet distance from it. This is, admittedly, more an escape route than a perfect solution. But whether there is or can be such a solution must, in my view, be open to doubt, since any attempt to reach one ends up trapped somewhere between past and present. Not by chance, then, do other studies of 'mixed families' also dwell in detail on the problem of language – and find only incomplete solutions to its hidden difficulties (e.g. Spickard 1989: 20, 22; Rosenblatt et al. 1995: 7).

The dilemma is evident enough. How can one write about classificatory terms used in society without employing those same terms? Is it not like trying to swim without getting your feet wet? It is another irony of history that the social scientist too cannot escape from history; indeed it is this which makes his or her work resemble the squaring of a circle. We can guess what traps, misunderstandings and reproaches are in store for us here. But the hope remains that, if we point out the traps, we can also find a way out of them. (This would be a kind of multicultural version of the Baron Münchhausen story. But what will prove stronger in the end: one's own bootstraps or the accumulated historical burden of terms associated with racial discrimination?)

The task is hardly made easier by the fact that the terms for particular groups also have their own history and problems. Take 'blacks', for example. When Robert K. Merton, one of the most renowned American sociologists, published an article in 1941 on 'Intermarriage and the social structure' (1976), he still employed the word 'Negro' as a matter of course. For us today, however, it is closely associated with discrimination and is virtually never used (except as an insult for the purpose of disparagement). But what is there instead? 'African American' is quite widespread, but it too can cause offence (if taken in an excluding sense to suggest that the person in question should go back to Africa). The most common term is 'black' – though it is not very precise and often has little to do with actual skin colour. Actually we always need inverted commas, because a 'black' is not necessarily black (rarely is, in fact), just as a 'white' is not truly white unless he or she happens to have been born an albino.

In short, all the terms have an emotional charge that refers to certain social and political constellations; they are locked into the mentality of a particular epoch. Here too, then, there are no simple solutions and controversy is always present.

And then there are Jews (or perhaps 'Jews' in inverted commas?). As we have seen, many assimilated Jews from the epoch before Hitler could give only a very vague idea of what was meant by the word (e.g. Hilde Domin, in Schultz 1986: 88), while afterwards it acquired new content for many from the common fate that had bonded Jews together in persecution. On the other hand, the same history means that many non-Jews feel uncomfortable or apprehensive about using the word; it reminds them of evil times in the past, it sounds like an insult – should one really be saying that? Some are surprised, almost reproachful, when they learn that Jews call themselves Jews. Isn't that racism? It is enough to make the confusion complete.

Gert Mattenklott's book *Über Juden in Deutschland* opens as follows:

> If someone in Germany starts speaking about Jews, the conversation usually stops – especially if a Jew is present. Among many other reasons for this, one will suffice: namely, that Germans have literally been left speechless in relation to Jews. Is 'Jew' not a term of insult? In a number of contexts, one can get round it by speaking of Israelis, but obviously not all Jews are Israelis nor even all Israelis Jews. Things become especially awkward with abstract words such as 'Judaism' or 'Jewishness'. Can one speak of Judaism and Germany as Novalis spoke of Christianity and

Europe? Should one believe in such a thing as 'Jewishness', after all the pain of renouncing Germanness as a collective destiny? When cornered, people seek refuge in 'Jewish people' or 'Jewish fellow citizens'. But new problems immediately arise. Who are Jewish? Those who profess the Mosaic faith? Offspring of eth-nically Jewish mothers? Members of a Jewish community? In the name of what do we still call someone Jewish who is ethnically only part-Jewish or who has been baptised a Chris-tian? (Mattenklott 1992: 9)

The term 'Aryan' has become even more suspect, because it directly recalls the core Nazi ideology of a 'Nordic master race'. But what follows from this? Are Jews still Jews *tout court* because the term refers to a social community (based on reli-gion or common destiny), whereas there are no 'Aryans' but only an ideological construction of ties of blood and biology (so let's please have additional terms to mark our distance from race doctrines)? All this at least suggests a marking out of the terrain.

The disputes are thus far from over – on the contrary, they are becoming still more explosive. To recapitulate: the old ethnic classifications carry within them a historical burden of discrimination. But what if minority groups themselves start wanting to rebuild, and attach themselves to, a history and identity of their own? Is this their response to loss and suppres-sion of their history? Or is it what Agnes Heller (1994) calls 'biopolitics', the erection of new fences and dividing lines? Does 'self-ethnicization' unleash a dynamic that leads to 'ethnic sep-aratism' (Neckel 1997)? Or is it the case that, although it initially – like other social movements – displays boundless energies, unbridled activity, restless experimentation and a large number of excesses, this is all just a passing phase on the road to self-definition in which minority groups first have to search for themselves?

Three decades have now passed since the rise of the black movement in the United States, and other ethnic groups too have long been seeking out and emphasizing their roots. Even those of mixed descent are starting to highlight rather than suppress their dual or multiple identity. It is in relation to just such efforts that controversy is flaring up today. Are the classifications used in this context the expression of a new consciousness? Or are they an attempt to create a new demarcation, even a new apartheid? Or are they perhaps both together, depending upon circumstances, audience and protagonists? More specifically, should the new formulas that permit – or should we say promote – ethnic self-classification be treated as a 'highly promising start'[14] or a new 'ghettoization'?[15]

Under the heading 'America is being ethnically mapped', John David Morley writes:

> The ethnic group column in official forms is to be enlarged, with the clever aim of reducing the number of *black–white* classificatory procedures. The wider range of ethnic options will make things more difficult for citizens, however. How black, or rather how Afro-American, am I really? How Judaeo-Hispanic? How Asian? People who have never before grappled with such notions will now have to look more closely. Actually, where did Grandfather come from? And Grandmother? In doubtful cases (and in the land of the melting pot the majority of cases are probably doubtful), what should I choose and what are the likely long-term consequences for my children and my children's children? With their well-intended enlargement of the list of possible ethnic affiliations, the US authorities have opened a Pandora's box.
>
> What is happening in America is also of great interest for Europe. All European countries have become lands of immigration, if only in the sense of the migration that has long been taking place within the frontiers of the European Union. To sum up the American experiment with new criteria, it would seem that attempts to find an identity inevitably lead to the question: 'What separates us from each other?', not: 'What do we have in common?' ... Early experiences of classifying the American people in ever smaller ethnic groups leave reason to fear that the danger of an unintended ghettoization might appear.[16]

Who is a German today?

These are the new questions emerging today. But for all the differing assessments, hopes and fears, it is clear that social-demographic trends alone have made ethnic classification increasingly complicated. In the age of mobility, mass transport and economic networking, a growing number of people work and live with others beyond the radius of their own group of origin; perhaps leave their native country for a short time or for ever (whether to escape poverty, famine and persecution, to gain education and work, or simply out of curiosity and a desire to travel); cross frontiers, are born here, grow up there, marry and have children somewhere else. In the case of the United States, this might become 'the new normal thing' in the twenty-first century: 'The number of bicultural partnerships is increasing, and so it is no longer a rarity to be both white and Asian, or Arab and Jewish.'[17] In Germany such mixed relationships are certainly less common, but here too the tendency is unmistakable.

In 1960, for example, those who married in the Federal Republic were nearly all German. Only in one out of twenty-five marriages was, to use the official formula, 'a foreigner involved' (that is, at least one of the couple had a foreign passport). In 1997, by contrast, nearly every fifth marriage was contracted 'by or with foreigners': that is, husband or wife or both were foreign citizens.[18]

The problem of social classification is especially acute in relation to this (fast-growing) group of migrants and their families. Where do they belong: to us or to others, and which others? It is a question here of varied, shifting, tangled lives, which resist incorporation into the established categories. They are people with exotic-sounding names, strange looks, different-coloured skin and hair, who trigger in us all the associations of distance and the Orient. And then they suddenly answer you in Bavarian or Schwabian dialect; it turns out that they grew up in the Kreuzberg area of Berlin or in Duisburg. In short, they challenge our images of normality and turn our expectations upside-down.

As we read in a novel by the British-Indian author Hanif Kureishi: 'Everyone looks at you ... and thinks: an Indian boy, how exotic, how interesting, what stories of aunties and elephants we'll hear now from him. And you're from Orpington' (1990: 141). In fact, the boy has never once been to India. The world is playing up. Nothing is as it seems to be. Who is what, who is who?

Similar stories can be told from Germany:

'Well now, Herr Kayankaya. So you're a private detective. Interesting name that – Kayankaya.'
  'Not so much interesting as Turkish.'
  'Ah!'
The smile becomes even sweeter, the eye slits hardly larger than razor blades.
  'Turkish. A Turkish private detective? So now there's one of everything. And how come you speak such good German, if I may presume to ask?'
  'Because I never learnt any other language. My parents died young and I grew up in a German family.'
  'But you are Turkish – I mean ... '
  'I have a German passport, if that puts your mind at rest.'
(Arjouni 1991: 7)

Such situations cause irritation and amazement in everyday life. They also give rise to complicated official procedures and discretionary rules, and naturally, because of the difficulty of the issues, to slips and errors. As we have seen, the question of who is black or Jewish involves a maze of regulations, criteria and interpretations, but now it turns out that the question 'Who is German?' is not so simple either. Instead we see the 'end of clarity' (Zygmunt Bauman) or a 'new obscurity' (Jürgen Habermas). Here is just one example, again taken from a 'mixed' family:

Georgios Chatzimarkakis had lived in Germany undisturbed for the last quarter of a century and, as a German-Greek holding dual citizenship, had begun a promising political career. Then came the ruling from the bureaucrats in Bonn: all these years, the newly started politician and prospective doctor in political science had not been a German citizen. The twenty-nine-year-old was told to hand over his German passport.... The real zigzag course between absurd definitions began when Chatzimarkakis decided to marry and an official at the registry office in Bonn asked for proof of citizenship from the man with the foreign-sounding name.

The son of a German and a Cretan set about looking for a document that would prove his naturalization. Having been born in Duisburg, he had always taken it for granted that he was a German. But until 1974 the rule had been that children with one foreign parent did not accede to citizenship. 'You can't possibly be a German!' Chatzimarkakis was told by an interior ministry official in the course of his investigations.

The official was right, as it turned out. At first the aliens office assumed that Chatzimarkakis had become a German by an act of official grace, because the Greek authorities had not recognized his father's marriage in Germany and the son would otherwise have been stateless. But when the papers arrived in Bonn from Duisburg, the bureaucrats found an obstacle on the back of a form: that is, the politician's father had subsequently had his son legitimized in Greece. The child had thus become a Greek in 1970 – which was reason enough for punctilious German officials to withdraw his German citizenship. His naturalization was cancelled, but the decision was inadvertently not passed on to other authorities.[19]

Many might think that there was a simple answer: a person's citizenship is shown on his or her passport, and so anyone who has a German passport is a German. But this assumption is, well, just too simple. A passport is by no means enough for someone to count as German for official purposes; other documents are required in addition. But the problem is (1) that it is not at all clear which documents and how many are necessary, and (2) that, in an age of migration, escapes and expulsions, war, unrest and political turmoil, many documents are burnt or lost, stolen or destroyed, and so not everyone has a complete set in their possession. The bureaucratic regulations basically expect the whole world to be as it is in contemporary Germany – orderly and well rubber-stamped. Anyone whose life has been

126

different – less orderly, not 100 per cent verifiable – can encounter many obstacles and perhaps end up in a blind alley,
German passport notwithstanding. Here is another case history
from a 'mixed' family.

District authority. Department II: district residents. Section I:
nationality. Subject: nationality matters. On the desk are the
papers of Citizen W. from Munich. What has the man done?
Some years ago he produced a daughter, who is now thinking of
pursuing a career as a doctor. But in order to take up a position
at a German hospital, the daughter needs proof that she is as
German as the hospital. In this context, thank goodness, it does
not count that Citizen W. ... once chose an Italian woman as his
wife and the mother of his daughter, for the mother, by virtue of
being a woman, is not relevant in matters pertaining to nationality. But the father! He is seventy-one years old. Born in Dres-
den. Served under the Supreme Commander of All Germans,
and for that spent time as a Soviet prisoner of war. Was a
teacher in the German Democratic Republic and was soon
incarcerated in the German Democratic Prison. Subsequently
ran away to the Western part of Berlin. Worked twenty-five
years for Bavarian Radio in Munich. Is he German? Well, now,
nobody knows anything for sure.

It is true that W. may somehow or other be German. At least
it does not directly count against him that he worked for ten
years at an American university; nor must the fact that at the
radio he was in charge of foreign-language broadcasts necessarily
be to his disadvantage. More serious is his lack of such and
such conclusive evidence that he is German. So what now?
Passport? Not enough. Identity card? Ridiculous. Birth certificate? Anyone can get hold of one. Album of family papers?
Come off it! What does Karl Thiem say on behalf of the district
authority? 'We don't intend to declare his citizenship invalid.'
But the issue is different when it comes to recognizing his
daughter's citizenship, which is derived from the father's.
After all, an indubitably German daughter needs a decidedly
German father, and the problem with W. is that he cannot
completely prove his existence over a period of decades.
Anyone, says Thiem, who was born before the Second World
War but has an identity card issued after 1945 does not,

unfortunately, prove anything with it; nor is a birth certificate by any means sufficient. How a German can conclusively demonstrate his or her Germanness – 'we have a whole department dealing with that,' says Thiem. In general there should be enough clues and papers – only there would have to be exactly the right number for the pieces of circumstantial evidence to condense into some kind of proof.[20]

The question of who has which citizenship is, of course, regulated by each country's citizenship laws. In Germany, unlike other countries, these place most weight on ancestry (*ius sanguinis*, literally 'blood law') and not on residence, birthplace or actual circumstances of life. In the age of 'transnational social spaces' (Pries 1996), however, such a way of handling things can no longer cover the realities of life for many people; it is even bound to create paradoxical situations, such as the recent choice of a Turkish woman as Miss Germany.[21] The anachronism of the current regulations is especially apparent from the example of the children of foreign workers. As one study concludes: 'Children of foreign workers recruited in the fifties, sixties and early seventies ... have made their home in Germany; ... they are geared to German norms and goals in life, have command of the German language, and in many cases can be regarded as foreigners only in a statistical sense' (Hermann 1995: 29). A new range of concepts and distinctions have been created in social science and politics to grasp at least some of the complexity of the new conditions. There is talk, for example, of 'indigenous foreigners' (Bade 1992: 393) and 'foreign Germans' (1992: 401), 'nationals with a foreign passport' (Nuscheler 1995: 113ff) and 'foreigners of German origin' (1995: 122ff), 'people brought up as Germans' and 'people brought up as foreigners' (Schmalz–Jacobsen and Hansen 1997: 186), of 'real foreigners' and 'foreigners only in the statistical sense' (Hradil 1995b: 292), 'settled foreigners' and 'quasi-foreigners' (Hallson 1996: 276–7), and last but not least of 'other Germans' (Mecheril and Teo 1994). Countless jokes are already circulating about the new crop of ethnic distinctions. After German unification, for example, there was this one playing on the views of East Germans held by West Germans: 'What is the difference between a Turk and a Saxon? Answer: The Turk speaks German and works for a living' (quoted in Geyer 1995: 227).

In spite of Germany's restrictive laws, however, many individuals or groups do finally manage to acquire citizenship; their status then changes, from 'foreigner' to 'national'. At the same time, upheavals such as the collapse of the former Eastern bloc have redrawn the political landscape, as some states have disappeared and others sprung up. This has changed many people's citizenship – from 'Czechoslovaks', for instance, to either 'Czechs' or 'Slovaks'. But, since any attempt at classification implies stable conditions, the spreading instability in the world provides new fuel for misunderstandings, misjudgements and other errors, including in the categories used for German statistics. Take the case of German marriage statistics, or rather those concerning 'mixed families' of Germans and foreigners. Anyone who reads these without bearing in mind the untidiness and instability of the age of globalization will come to quite a few wrong conclusions. Many categories can mean things other than they appear to at first sight; they require interpretation and can really be decoded only with a knowledge of the vicissitudes of politics and history. Let us digress a little here to consider this point more closely.

The vagaries of international marriage and family statistics

In the last few decades, we have seen again and again how wars, political upheavals and world economic downturns create typical patterns in binational marriage. After the Second World War, for example, there was a rise in the number of marriages between US military men and German women; in the 1980s German men began increasingly to marry women from economically underprivileged countries, especially the Philippines and Thailand; and since the collapse of the Eastern bloc there has been a new shift in the marriage market, so that German men now tend to wed more women from Eastern Europe (e.g. Heine-Wiedemann and Ackermann 1992; Lenz et al. 1993).

129

The precise scale of the increase is a most interesting question for theories of an international 'marriage market', but the published data make it difficult to give more than an approximate answer. Surprisingly enough, German Statistical Office figures show that, whereas in 1987 a total of 1,207 German men married women from Yugoslavia, increasing in 1991 to 1,778, the year 1993 saw only 1,145 marriages with women from 'the former Yugoslavia' (as the area was by then known). What was the reason for this fluctuation, for this decline instead of the expected further increase? A Statistical Office survey produced at least part of the explanation: namely, that the category 'former Yugoslavia' included only persons presenting a Yugoslav passport. Those who had had their passport endorsed as 'Slovenian' or 'Croatian' instead were recorded in German marriage statistics as coming from 'the rest of Europe' – and they vanished there. Similarly, the changed political circumstances meant that the category 'Soviet Union' was broken down into separate new categories, so that individuals became 'Russian', 'Belorussian', 'Ukrainian', and so on. One imagines that this did not make it easier to draw comparisons over time.

May it also be the case that German men involved in such marriages tend to be 'less German', and their foreign partners less 'foreign', than a naïve gaze would reveal? At a seminar I gave on the theme of 'binational marriages', where we were discussing the new pattern of marriages between German men and East European women, one student (a Romanian–German, as it happened) protested that some of the marriages were an artificial statistical creation. For there were many cases of young men from long-established German settlements in Eastern Europe who left for Germany, acquired German citizenship, then took a bride from their former homeland and settled down in Germany – a marriage whose record in the official statistics as binational (German–Romanian, for example) hardly corresponded to the reality. A man and a woman close to each other in history and ancestry were separated by the logic of statistics and turned into mutual 'foreigners'.

To complicate matters a little further, the age of globalization means that many people have not just one passport but two at the same time. Such persons with dual citizenship create new problems of political categorization, as it is not clear whether they should appear in the population figures as nationals or as foreigners. Special regulations have been developed for these cases and, after what has been said, it will not surprise the reader that these involve paradoxes of their own. Children of German–Spanish marriages, for example, 'usually acquire both citizenships and appear in German statistics as Germans, in Spanish ones as Spanish' (Thränhardt 1995: 5). One has to be aware of this and other practices to interpret correctly the results that they produce. For of the five major national groups living in Germany, Spaniards are 'the only group whose number, according to German statistics, is growing smaller year by year' (1995: 5). But the reason for this is that there are numerous German–Spanish marriages and the children from them appear in German statistics only as German. If we were to take the Spanish statistics, the results would look very different.

Let us conclude this digression by briefly mentioning something else pointed out by a student at a seminar on binational marriages. This student, herself coming from a German–Greek family, had two passports and citizenships, as did her sister. When the two of them went on a trip together to England, she took her Greek passport because she had just mislaid her German one, while her sister travelled on her German passport. Upon returning to Germany, the 'German' sister was quickly waved through, but the 'Greek' was subjected to thorough questioning.

Living between cultures

The fast-growing groups of people in 'mixed' families do not only pose a problem of social classification. From each country's point of view, there is also more and more the question of the internal order: that is, of the rules by which such people are to go about their daily lives. The reason why this has become so significant is immediately apparent if we compare the present with earlier epochs.

Towards the Multicultural Family

When a man and a woman entered into marriage in pre-industrial society, they nearly always had in common a large repertoire of experiences, value judgements, ways of living, and so on. For the world of everyday life was then far more closed than it is today, and marriage opportunities were greatly limited by factors ranging from class and property to ethnic origin and religion. In comparison, the everyday world of today is much more thoroughly mixed: people from different regions and social strata meet and often marry one another. The old barriers erected by the law or by the wider family have not completely disappeared, but they are much weaker than they used to be. The principle of a free choice of partner has become generally accepted, so that people who come together (with or without a marriage certificate) often have quite different backgrounds. Or, as Berger and Kellner put it in a classic text, the modern choice of partner is characterized by the meeting of two strangers:

> Marriage in our society is a *dramatic* act in which two strangers come together and redefine themselves. ... the term 'strangers' [does not] mean, of course, that the candidates for the marriage come from widely discrepant social backgrounds – indeed, the data indicate that the contrary is the case. The strangeness rather lies in the fact that, unlike marriage candidates in many previous societies, those in ours typically come from different face-to-face contexts. (1965: 222–3)

The marital relation thereby acquires new meaning, but also, of course, new strains. For the great opportunity of personally chosen togetherness – namely, the creation of a common world beyond the legacy of family and kin – requires that both participants make enormous contributions. Within the system of modern marriage, the partners are not only expected to construct their own form of togetherness; they *must* do so:

> Marriage and the family used to be firmly embedded in a matrix of wider community relationships. ... There were few separating barriers between the world of the individual family and the

wider community. ... The same social life pulsated through the house, the street and the community. ... In our contemporary society, by contrast, each family constitutes its own segregated sub-world. ... This fact requires a much greater effort on the part of the marriage parties. Unlike in earlier situations in which the establishment of the new marriage simply added to the differentiation and complexity of an already existing social world, the marriage partners now are embarked on the often difficult task of constructing for themselves the little world in which they live. (Berger and Kellner 1965: 225)

This is especially true of binational or bicultural couples, where each partner comes from a different country or culture. Such unions also existed in earlier epochs, of course, but their number has increased considerably in recent times. Owing to migration of labour, political upheavals and political persecution, mass tourism and foreign travel for education or business, every sixth marriage in Germany is now nationally mixed.[22] What Berger and Kellner saw as characteristic of modern marriage is now even more applicable. For in nationally mixed marriages the strangers are 'stranger and the differences in socialization are greater' (Hardach-Pinke 1988: 116).

Today, in every marriage, different lifestyles, values, ways of thinking and communicating, rituals and daily routines have to be fitted together into one family world. In the case of binational/bicultural marriages, this means that both partners must achieve the 'construction of a new intercultural reality' (Hardach-Pinke 1988: 217), build an 'intercultural lifeworld'[23] or a 'binational family culture' (Scheibler 1992: 87ff). They act within a space that has been little structured beforehand, as two different worlds meet within it. In this situation, for which there is no preparation and no definite rules, the partners have to work out arrangements of their own (1992: 45).

Much that used simply to happen, without any questions asked, must now be weighed up and decided upon. Where shall we live: in your country or mine, or perhaps in a third where neither has the advantage of it being home? Shall we stay here all the time or later move to your home country? Who has which opportunities where? Who must bear which burdens where? Who will be without legal status, job protection or pension cover? Is agreement to be reached in your language or mine, or in a third, or in whichever suits the occasion? Which festivals and holidays will we celebrate? What shall we do about family visits and all the many branches of the family? What about the division of labour at home? How are the children to be brought up: in your religion or mine, in your language or mine? What forenames will we choose, reflecting which of our origins?

To repeat: there are no models for any of these decisions. Each couple goes its own way, seeks its own forms. Whether they choose to follow one or the other cultural tradition in its entirety; whether they try to find forms combining elements from both; whether they test out several options and perhaps keep switching around (Scheibler 1992: 44ff) – all this will depend on their personal history, on where they now live and what plans they have for the future, as well as on the values and discrimination patterns of their respective environments. This is how each binational couple lives out its own history, its own distinctive version of binational family culture.

Finally, a binational/bicultural marriage also makes both partners confront their own origins, with sometimes paradoxical results. Someone who looked for the attraction of 'the other' in a relationship with a foreigner suddenly discovers the 'German' element in his or her own self. 'One sees how deeply rooted is one's own value system – indeed, in many respects one sees it for the first time' (Elschenbroich 1988: 368). Especially when one thinks of the children and their future, memories will come back with particular force, making it necessary to confront one's own socialization and previous history, values and desires – one's own identity. The question 'Who am I, what do I want?' is posed anew in the course of a binational marriage. And it leads on to further questions that call for a crucial decision: 'What do I want to keep?', 'What can I give up?', 'What is important to me?'

Binational couples more than others are thus repeatedly forced into decisions which may place them under constant strain or at worst lead to the breakdown of their relationship. On the other hand, this offers them the chance to remain more open with each other in everyday life, and to risk new starts over and over again. 'When it works out well, something is preserved over the years from the original audacity of optimistic experimentation; then binational marriages are especially lively and interesting' (Elschenbroich 1988: 366).

Cautious hope

The increase in 'more colourful', mixed families is viewed quite differently according to the observer's perspective. On the one hand, it is often the case that those who choose to marry someone 'different' or 'foreign' meet with suspicion and mistrust. But, on the other hand, there is also another picture of such people as bold, open-minded bearers of tolerance and understanding – in short, as pioneers of the multicultural society.

Evidently the first image feeds off xenophobic prejudices. The second may be more attractive, but that does not necessarily mean it is right. It overlooks the fact that such relationships do not develop solely out of love but – just like other relationships – out of a mixture of motives. And it overlooks the fact that people in such relationships are not made of eternal angelic tolerance but have their own feelings of fear, hurt and bigotry. To put it more provocatively: the subject of racism in bicultural relationships would be worth a separate investigation.

Nevertheless, despite such reservations, I would like to end by risking a note of cautious confidence about the future. Life in a bicultural family, because it cannot be inserted into the normal parameters, is a life involving biographical uncertainty. Now, biographical uncertainty can be troublesome and irritating; it can make people fearful and lead them to adapt. But it can also throw up new experiences and viewpoints. 'Inspiration' can develop out of the inner turmoil – as Kafka once wrote in relation to his generation of Jewish writers and his own personal experience.[24] A topical example would be the writers from various corners of the former British empire who, in recent years, have taken English letters by storm, broken through the prevailing tedium and weary scepticism, and transformed 'the English language with bright colours and strange cadences and foreign eyes' (Iyer 1993: 50):

> The Booker Prize is London's way of formally commemorating and coronating literary tradition.... In 1981 the Booker went to Salman Rushdie's tumultuous, many-headed myth of modern India, *Midnight's Children*. [Since then], it has been given to two Australians, a part Maori, a South African, a woman of Polish descent, a Nigerian and an exile from Japan.... [In 1997] the $30,000 award was shared by Barry Unsworth, an Englishman married to a Finn and living in Italy...; and Michael Ondaatje, a Sri Lankan of Indian, Dutch and English ancestry, educated in Britain, long resident in Canada, with siblings on four continents.... Five days earlier, the Nobel Prize for Literature had been awarded to Derek Walcott, a poet of African, Dutch and English descent, born in St Lucia and commuting these days between Boston and Trinidad – a 'divided child', in his own words. (1993: 50)

These are a new group of 'translated men', to quote Salman Rushdie (in Iyer 1993: 50), who is one of them himself. They share a 'hyphenated existence' and the hope that the string will reach between the worlds: that they will be able to take what they need and want from every conceivable tradition:

> All are situated at a crossroads from which they can reflect, and reflect on, the new forms and Mississippi masalas of our increasingly small, increasingly mongrel, increasingly mobile global village. Indians writing of a London that is more like Bombay than Bombay, Japanese novelists who cannot read Japanese novels, Chinese women evoking a China they have seen only in their mothers' stories – all are amphibians who do not have an old home and a new home so much as two half-homes simultaneously. All are defined, in some ways, by being indefinable. (Iyer 1993: 52)

From a sociological point of view, we might say that these new aboriginals of the global village do not crumble under the ongoing pressure to classify them, but gain strength from the constant friction. Given favourable conditions, they can be vivid examples of the positive side of individualization, of the opportunities contained in 'risky freedoms' (Beck and Beck-Gernsheim 2001). Biographical uncertainty, understood in this way, always has two sides to it. It can be a burden, but it can also free people – for playing around with fixed categories, for sharpening their gaze, perhaps also for laughter, the most disarming of all weapons. It can spur people on to become 'disturbers of the peace' (a term used by Reich-Ranicki (1993) for the role of Jews in German literature).

Walter White, an American of mixed descent, once described as follows the experience that formed him: 'I am white and I am black, and know that there is no difference. Each casts a shadow, and all shadows are dark' (1969: 366). Perhaps, if experiences of this kind catch on, what Michael Walzer once said will come true: 'If identities become multiple, the passions will be spread around... and the earth will begin to look a less dangerous place' (1992: 136).

There is both historical and contemporary material to support the hope hinted at here. For example, studies of 'mixed families' show that many who live in them begin to perceive their surroundings anew through the experiences of their partner and children and to rebel against what they have grown accustomed to (e.g. Rosenblatt et al. 1995: 215ff; Alibhai-Brown and Montague 1992: *passim*). They learn to see – not only overt discrimination but also the fine web of muted prejudice, barely expressed judgements, barely conscious bigotry, which is taken for granted in everyday life. Let us recall for a moment the 'Rosenstrasse women's protest' in February 1943, a spectacular and successful act of resistance under National Socialism,[25] when several hundred people (most of them 'Aryans' living in mixed marriages) gathered in the middle of a Berlin street and chanted slogans to demand the release of husbands and children awaiting deportation. Not only did other 'Aryan' relatives and friends (some from well-established families) turn out in their support; there were also noblemen, a soldier in Wehrmacht uniform, even a woman wearing the golden insignia of the Nazi Party, the wife of the mayor of Potsdam, whose sister was married to a Jew.

Examples such as this give you some idea of why people who move between cultures and nations really do constitute a problem of order, in one sense at least. For they might infect others with their 'recalcitrance' – and this makes them 'unreliable' and suspicious. They are a source of danger, seedbeds of resistance. They may dare to look across the frontiers, to see through their arbitrary and random nature, to resist the power of habit. That makes them a nuisance. That is subversion.

Might they, the ones who do not belong, here and there burst the 'iron cage of serfdom'? That would be truly impertinent and unforgivable – if indeed they were to succeed.

Notes

Preface to the English Edition

1   Talcott Parsons, 'Religion in postindustrial society', *Action, Theory and the Human Condition* (New York: Free Press, 1978), p. 321.
2   *The Economist*, 31 January 1998, p. 43.

Chapter 1   The New Confusion about the Family

1   Gary Younge, 'On first-name terms only', *Guardian*, 19 June 1996, p. 9.
2   Maureen Freely, 'What do you call yours?', *Sybil*, 1, March 1998.
3   Anja Dilk, 'Das neue Namesrecht in der Praxis: Grosses Durcheinander', *Die Zeit*, 12 May 1995, p. 77.
4   'The year 1980 was to be the "Year of the Family", to be celebrated by a White House Conference on the subject. It was during the endless seminars and colloquia preparing this Conference that the question of definition surfaced dramatically. During this preparatory period, a radical semantic shift took place in the definition of the family.... The change was from speaking about *the family* to speaking about *families*. At first glance, this may seem an innocent shift, from the singular to the plural.... Upon closer scrutiny, the shift reveals itself as anything but innocent. It gave governmental recognition to precisely the kind of moral relativism

that has infuriated and mobilized large numbers of Americans' (Berger and Berger 1983: 59).

5 'In the 1950s and 1960s the sociological concept of lifestyles practically did not yet exist. One spoke of "family" and "the sociology of the family". After all, more than nine-tenths of the relevant age groups in Germany were married, and more than nine-tenths of these had children. But the growing differentiation in the structure of ordinary lives together then necessitated a "further conceptual roofing". Since the concept of the family ... could hardly be extended – or anyway, not so as to take in people living alone and non-marital forms of living together – a more abstract conceptualization became necessary and took shape precisely in the concept of "lifestyles"' (Hradil 1996: 61–2).

6 On what follows here, see Frevert (1996).

Chapter 2   When Divorce Becomes Normal

Some sections of this chapter borrow arguments that were first developed in Beck-Gernsheim (1996b). For the opening epigraphs, see J. Schmid (1989: 10) and Wolf Wondratschek, 'Die Ehe', *Süddeutsche Zeitung*, 13 November 1996, p. 13.

1 Statistisches Bundesamt (1995b: 109); Statistisches Bundesamt, *Arbeitsunterlage*, VIIB–181, 18 August 1999.

2 Ibid.

3 Since 1972, when an (incomplete) estimate was first made of the number of long-term non-marital relationships, the figure has risen nearly tenfold in West Germany from 137,000 to 1,500,000 in 1998 – to which should be added a further 500,000 for Eastern Germany: Statistisches Bundesamt (1995a: 24); *BiB-Mitteilungen* (published by the Bundesinstitut für Bevölkerungsforschung (BiB) beim Statistischen Bundesamt), 2 (1999), p. 12.

4 The survey investigated only cohabiting couples and thus excluded long-term relationships in separate dwellings (Vaskovics and Rupp 1995: 26). It is by no means obvious that this is the best focus, since it produces a selective effect in the direction of stability. It does not apply anyway to the study conducted by the German Youth Institute (Tölke 1991: 120).

5 Diekmann and Engelhardt regard children and home ownership, among others, as marital investments.

6 See the argument that Cherlin (1992: 16) and Hall (1996) develop to explain similar findings in the USA and Canada.

7 From a discussion among children of separated parents, quoted from Stierlin and Duss-von-Werdt (1995: 125).

8 See, for example, Jopt (1997) and Cherlin and Furstenberg (1986: 136 ff), ch. 6, 'Grandparents and divorce'.

9 On what follows, see Reberg (1997) and Napp-Peters (1995).

10 Zygmunt Bauman, 'Wir sind wie Landstreicher – die Moral im Zeitalter der Beliebigkeit', *Süddeutsche Zeitung*, 16–17 November 1993, p. 17.

11 The title of a film by Wolfgang Becker that came out in 1997.

12 On the concept of 'do-it-yourself' biography, see Beck and Beck-Gernsheim (1993) and Beck and Beck-Gernsheim (2001).

Chapter 3   Life as a Planning Project

1 For a more detailed account, see Beck and Beck-Gernsheim (1993) and Beck and Beck-Gernsheim (2001).

2 Such an idea of individualization is implied by Ilona Ostner and Peter Boy (1991: 18), who then proceed to do battle with the very concept.

3 This idea of individualization is implied by Karl Ulrich Mayer (1991: 89), who then similarly uses it to do battle with the very concept.

4 *International Herald Tribune*, 11 December 1989; *Süddeutsche Zeitung*, 10 September 1990 and 27 August 1991.

5 *Der Spiegel* 14, (1990), pp. 162–8.

6 Peter de Thier, 'Goldene Zukunft durch Ehevertrag – für Anwälte', *Süddeutsche Zeitung*, 27 August 1991.

7 From interview material in Schindele (1990: 66).

8 This is the case among one group whose strongly traditional conduct in life would hardly make one suspect it: namely, orthodox Jews. The background is as follows. Tay–Sachs disease, a hereditary disorder with serious consequences, is quite common among Ashkenazi Jews, and they are vigorously urged to have a genetic test before marrying. If this shows that both partners are bearers of the Tay–Sachs gene, there is a considerable risk that the illness will affect their eventual children, and so they are strongly advised not to go ahead with the marriage: Merz (1987); Richards (1996: 263).

9 *Der Spiegel* 10, (1997), p. 237, quoting from *The Lancet*.

Chapter 4   Generational Contract and Gender Relations

This chapter develops and updates ideas first presented in the essay 'Generation und Geschlecht' (Beck-Gernsheim 1996a).

1   In the GDR, the normative model of motherhood was markedly different. Whereas the prevailing idea in West Germany was that, at least in the early years of life, the child needs as much maternal care as possible, in the East it was not only defined as socially and politically desirable but also broadly accepted among the population that the mother should resume her job quite soon after the birth of a child. Public forms of childcare were regarded not as suspect or potentially harmful to the child, but as a normal part of life for women, children and families. Nothing much has changed in this model in the new Eastern *Länder* of the Federal Republic, where women have hardly let themselves be swayed by images of uncaring mothers who go out to work. The generation that frequented creches, kindergartens and nurseries mostly wants the same model for its own children (Schröter 1996; Hildebrandt and Wittmann 1996). Whether this wish is being fulfilled is another question, however, as many childcare facilities were closed down after unification.

2   In the *Süddeutsche Zeitung*, for instance, there was a weekly column called 'Neues vom Hausmann' ('News from the man who stays at home'), selections from which have recently appeared as a book (Makowsky 1996). Also in *Die Zeit*, new fathers have made their experiences known to the broad public. See Thomas Hallet, 'Erster Tag mit Leonie', *Die Zeit*, 31, 28 July 1995, p. 55; and Reinhard Schlieker, 'Daa-da-daa-da-daa', *Die Zeit*, 34, 18 August 1995, p. 54.

3   Calculated for the year 1995 from Statistisches Bundesamt 1997.

4   Figure for the year 1995, from Statistisches Bundesamt, Fachserie 1, Reihe 3: *Haushalte und Familie*, 1995.

5   Ellen Goodman, 'A perpetual rush hour for baby boomers', *International Herald Tribune*, 14 September 1995, p. 11.

6   On the following, see Beck-Gernsheim (1997b).

7   For calculations of the needs in question, see Hradil (1995a: 153); Rosenkranz (1996: 214 ff).

8   Giddens (1994a: 190), alluding to Howard Glennerster's *Paying for Welfare* (Oxford: Blackwell, 1985).

9 From a speech given on 9 December 1996 at the Wissenschafts-zentrum in Bonn, and quoted here from *BiB-Mitteilungen,* 1 (1997), p. 30.

Chapter 5   We Want a Special Child

This chapter develops ideas that were first put forward in 'Vom Kinderwunsch zum Wunschkind' (Beck-Gernsheim 1997c).

1 'In families with a genetic risk, the aim should be to give human genetic advice before conception. If necessary... prophylactic measures should be aimed for' (Bach et al. 1990: 41).

2 These formulations are quoted from a fact-sheet that the Freiburg gynaecologist M. Schulte-Vallentin handed out to his patients.

3 Here, for example, is Hubert Markl, former president of the Deutsche Forschungsgemeinschaft, in a lecture on 'Genetics and Ethics': 'I want to state very clearly – because the opposite is sometimes argued – that to renounce for such reasons the idea of having children of one's own is at least as praiseworthy as the decision taken out of relentlessly fatalistic piety to allow a possibly cruel fate to take its course' (Markl 1989).

4 In a publication of the charity Support after Termination for Abnormality, we read: 'The decision to terminate a wanted baby because of foetal abnormality is one made out of care for the unborn child' (quoted from McNally 1995: 142).

5 Lord Justice Stephenson interpreted the legal provision for abor-tion in the event of genetic foetal abnormality as follows: 'That paragraph may have been added in the interests of the mother, the family and the general public, but I would prefer to believe that its main purpose, if not its sole purpose, was to benefit the unborn child' (quoted from McNally 1995: 142).

6 In 1991 a total of 42,745 prenatal investigations (amniocenteses or choriobiopsies) were carried out in West Germany; in 1995 the figure was already 61,794 (according to Irmgard Nippert at the conference 'Ratlosigkeit trotz Informationsfülle? Schwan-gerschaftsberatung vor den Herausforderungen der modernen Medizin', Wissenschaftszentrum Bonn, June 1997).

7 Interview with James Watson in *Focus*, 17 (1993), pp. 94–7; retranslated.

8 *Abendzeitung*, 11 March 1997, pp. 1,6.

9 *The Economist*, 8 January 1994, pp. 15–16.

10 See, for example, 'Safe semen', *Newsweek*, 12 February 1989, p. 7; 'Not the right father', *Newsweek*, 13 March 1990, pp. 50–1.
11 'Samenbanken – Gefährliche Spende', *Der Spiegel*, 34, (1997), p. 159.

Chapter 6   Towards the Multicultural Family

This chapter is based on the article 'Schwarze Juden und griechische Deutsche. Ethnische Zuordnung im Zeitalter der Globalisierung' (Beck-Gernsheim 1998). For the purposes of this book, it has been abridged at some points and expanded at others.

1 See Vera Graaf, 'Die Aussenhaut des Theaters. Ein New Yorker Streit über die Rassentrennung im Drama', *Süddeutsche Zeitung*, 14 February 1997, p. 11.
2 J. Schuhler, 'Ich bin weder schwarz noch weiss, ich bin kunterbunt. Portrait über Amadeo Richardson' (Munich: BR-Fernsehproduktion 1992).
3 On what follows, see esp. Davis (1991) and Spickard (1989).
4 *International Herald Tribune*, 26 April 1984.
5 See, for example, contributions by several authors to Schultz (1986).
6 If the 'Aryan' partner in a 'privileged mixed marriage' died, this took away the last vestiges of protection for the Jewish partner. If the children from a 'privileged mixed marriage' left Germany and joined the foreign emigration, the parents' marriage was no longer 'privileged' but merely 'simple'.
7 This heading is an allusion to Ilse Aichinger's famous novel *Die grössere Hoffnung* (Aichinger 1976), whose main character, the girl Ellen, comes from a marriage between a Jewish mother and a non-Jewish father. She is therefore a 'wasted child. Her mother has emigrated and her father has reported for duty. And when she meets him, she must not speak of the mother.... There is obviously something not right about the grandparents too. Two are in the right, two in the wrong' (1976: 34–5).
8 The poet Gottfried Benn, for example, was accused of being Jewish because a colleague of his considered 'Benn' to be a Jewish family name (see Brückner 1980: 120).
9 Jean Améry in Schultz (1986: 68–9 and 72).
10 Hilde Domin in Schultz (1986: 88–9).

11 Michael Landmann in Schultz (1986: 116 and 120–2); emphasis in the original.

12 *Der Spiegel*, 22 (1996), pp. 22–5, and 25 (1996), p. 19; Julius Schoeps, 'Ostjuden unerwünscht?', *Allgemeine Jüdische Wochenzeitung*, 27 June 1996, p. 1.

13 According to Irene Kohlhaas, German ambassador to the former Soviet Republic of Moldavia, quoted from *Der Spiegel*, 22 (1996), p. 25.

14 *Süddeutsche Zeitung*, magazine supplement, 24 November 1995, p. 4.

15 John David Morley, 'Inländer und Ausländer. Amerika wird ethnisch kartographiert', *Süddeutsche Zeitung*, 28 April 1995, p. 11.

16 Ibid., emphasis in the original.

17 Richard Chaim Schneider, 'Minorität und Minoritäten. Schwarze Juden in den USA', *Süddeutsche Zeitung*, 3 July 1995.

18 For 1960 see Statistisches Bundesamt (1995a: 26); for 1997, Statistisches Bundesamt (1999), *Arbeitsunterlage*, VIIB – 177/103, Tabelle 5.1: 'Eheschliessungen nach der Staatsangehörigkeit der Ehepartner'.

19 Hans Monath, 'Sie sind ja gar kein Deutscher!', *Tageszeitung*, 27 July 1995, p. 1.

20 Michael Knopf, 'Die späte Identitätskrise des deutschen Bürgers W.', *Süddeutsche Zeitung*, 26–27 August 1995, p. 53.

21 *International Herald Tribune*, 20–21 February 1996, p. 5.

22 According to official statistics, a total of 417,420 marriages took place in Germany in 1998. In 66,050 of these, or 15.8 per cent, the two partners were of different nationalities (calculated from Statistisches Bundesamt, Fachserie 1, Reihe 1 (1998), Tabelle 8.12: 'Eheschliessungen nach der Staatsangehörigkeit der Ehepartner'). But in reality the number of binational marriages should be higher, since the official figures include only those recorded at a German registry office, not those which took place abroad or at the consulate of a foreign country in Germany.

23 As in the title of Hardach-Pinke (1988).

24 In June 1921 Kafka wrote in a letter to Max Brod: 'Most young Jews who began to write German wanted to leave Jewishness behind them, and their father approved of this, but vaguely (this vagueness was what was outrageous to them). But with their posterior legs they were still glued to their father's Jewishness and with their anterior legs they found no new ground. The

ensuing despair became their inspiration.' *Franz Kafka, Letters to Friends, Family, and Editors* (New York: Schocken Books, 1977), p. 289; quoted in German in Reich-Ranicki (1993: 29).

25 Stolzfus (1989, 1996); Jochheim (1993); *Der Spiegel*, 8 (1993), pp. 58–68.

References

Aichinger, Ilse 1963: *Herod's Children*. New York: Atheneum.
—— 1976: *Die grössere Hoffnung*. Frankfurt/Main: Fischer.
Alibhai-Brown, Yasmin, and Montague, Anne 1992: *The Colour of Love: mixed race relationships*. London: Virago.
Arjouni, Jakob 1991: *'Ein Mann, ein Mord.' Ein Kayankaya-Roman*. Zurich: Diogenes.
Bach, H., Göhler, W., Körner, H., Metzke, H., Schöneich, J., and Steinbicker, V. 1990: 'Orientierung humangenetischer Betreuung – genetische Beratung in der DDR'. *Medizinische Genetik*, 4, 40–2.
Bade, Klaus J. 1992: 'Paradox Bundesrepublik: Einwanderungssituation ohne Einwanderungsland'. In Klaus J. Bade (ed.), *Deutsche im Ausland, Fremde in Deutschland. Migration in Geschichte und Gegenwart*. Munich: Beck.
Badura, Bernhard (ed.) 1981: *Soziale Unterstützung und chronische Krankheit*. Frankfurt: Suhrkamp.
Beck, Ulrich 1986a: *Risikogesellschaft. Auf dem Weg in einer andere Moderne*. Frankfurt: Suhrkamp.
—— 1986b: *Risk Society: towards a new modernity*. London: Sage.
—— 1994: 'The reinvention of politics: towards a theory of reflexive modernization'. In Ulrich Beck, Anthony Giddens and Scott Lash, *Reflexive Modernization*. Cambridge: Polity, 1–55.
Beck, Ulrich, and Beck-Gernsheim, Elisabeth 1990: *Das ganz normale Chaos der Liebe*. Frankfurt: Suhrkamp.
—— 1993: 'Nicht Autonomie, sondern Bastelbiographie'. *Zeitschrift für Soziologie*, 22, 3 (June), 178–87.
—— 1995: *The Normal Chaos of Love*. Cambridge: Polity.

References

—— 2001: *Individualization. Institutionalized Individualism and its Social and Political Consequences*. London: Sage.

Beck, Ulrich, Vossenkuhl, Wilhelm, and Erdmann Ziegler, Ulf 1995: *Eigenes Leben: Ausflüge in die unbekannte Gesellschaft, in die wir leben*. Munich: Bayerische Rückversicherung Aktiengesellschaft.

Beck-Gernsheim, Elisabeth 1983: 'Vom "Dasein für Andere" zum Anspruch auf ein Stück "eigenes Leben"'. *Soziale Welt*, 3, 307–40.

—— 1989: *Mutterwerden – der Sprung in ein anderes Leben*. Frankfurt: Fischer.

—— 1996a: 'Generation und Geschlecht'. In Eckart Liebau and Christoph Wolf (eds), *Generation. Versuche über eine pädagogisch-anthropologische Grundbedingung*. Weinheim: Deutscher Studien-verlag, 24–41.

—— 1996b: 'Nur der Wandel ist stabil. Zur Dynamik der Familienentwicklung'. *Familiendynamik*, 3, 284–304.

—— 1997a: *Die Kinderfrage. Frauen zwischen Kinderwunsch und Unabhängigkeit*, 3rd edn. Munich: Beck.

—— 1997b: 'Geburtenrückgang und Kinderwunsch – die Erfahrung in Ost-Deutschland'. *Zeitschrift für Bevölkerungswissenschaft*, 1, 59–71.

—— 1997c: 'Vom Kinderwunsch zum Wunschkind'. In Eckart Liebau (ed.), *Generationen*. Munich: Juventa, 107–21.

—— 1998: 'Schwarze Juden und griechische Deutsche. Ethnische Zuordnung im Zeitalter der Globalisierung'. In Ulrich Beck (ed.), *Perspektiven der Weltgesellschaft*. Frankfurt: Suhrkamp, 125–67.

Berger, Brigitte, and Berger, Peter L. 1983: *The War over the Family: Capturing the Middle Ground*. New York: Anchor Press.

—— 1984: *In Verteidigung der bürgerlichen Familie*. Reinbek: Rowohlt.

Berger, Peter, Berger, Brigitte, and Kellner, Hansfried 1975: *Das Unbehagen in der Modernität*. Frankfurt: Fischer.

Berger, Peter L. and Kellner, Hansfried 1965: 'Die Ehe und die Konstruktion der Wirklichkeit'. *Soziale Welt*, 3, 220–5.

Bertram, Hans 1994: 'Die Stadt, das Individuum und das Verschwinden der Familie'. *Aus Politik und Zeitgeschichte*, 29–30, 22 July, 15–35.

Biel, Maria 1995: 'Ähnlichkeit mit lebenden Personen erwünscht'. *Süddeutsche Zeitung*, magazine supplement, 5–6 January, 28–32.

Blasius, Dirk 1992: *Ehescheidung in Deutschland im 19. und 20. Jahrhundert*. Frankfurt: Fischer.

Blatt, Robin J. 1991: *Bekomme ich ein gesundes Kind? Chancen und Risiken der vorgeburtlichen Diagnostik*. Reinbek: Rowohlt.

148

References

Borscheid, Peter 1988: 'Zwischen privaten Netzen und öffentlichen Institutionen. Familienumwelten in historischer Perspektive'. In Deutsches Jugendinstitut (ed.), *Wie geht's der Familie? Ein Handbuch zur Situation der Familien heute*. Munich: Kösel, 272–80.

Boston, Sarah 1994: *Too Deep for Tears*. London: Pandora.

Boston Women's Health Book Collective, The 1987: *Unser Körper, unser Leben*, vol. 2. Reinbek: Rowohlt.

Braach, Mile 1994: *Rückblende. Erinnerungen einer Neunzigjährigen*. Frankfurt: Fischer.

Bradish, Paula, Gräning, Gisela, and Kratz, Tina 1993: *Reproduktionsmedizin, Gentechnologie, Pränatale Diagnostik und ihre Bedeutung für Frauen. Eine Bestandsaufnahme zur Situation in Hamburg. Bericht im Auftrag des Senatamtes für Gleichstellung der Freien und Hansestadt Hamburg*. Hamburg: Senatsamt für die Gleichstellung.

Bräutigam, Hans Harald, and Mettler, Liselotte 1985: *Die programmierte Vererbung*. Hamburg: Hoffmann und Campe.

Brothers, Joyce 1985: *What Every Woman Ought to Know about Love and Marriage*. New York: Ballantine Books.

Brückner, Peter 1980: *Das Abseits als sicherer Ort. Kindheit und Jugend Zwischen 1933 und 1945*. Berlin: Wagenbach.

Bundesinstitut für Bevölkerungsforschung 2000: *Bevölkerung. Fakten – Trends – Ursachen – Erwartungen*. Wiesbaden.

Bundesministerium für Familie und Seniorum (BMFS) 1994: *Fünfter Familienbericht. Familien und Familienpolitik im geeinten Deutschland*. Bonn.

Bundesministerium für Familie, Senioren, Frauen und Jugend (BMFSFJ) 1997: *Optionen der Lebensgestaltung junger Ehen und Kinderwunsch. Verbundsstudie – Endbericht*. Stuttgart: Kohlhammer.

Bundesministerium für Familie, Senioren, Frauen und Jugend (BMFSFJ) and Statistisches Bundesamt 1995: *Wo bleibt die Zeit? Die Zeitverwendung der Bevölkerung in Deutschland*. Wiesbaden.

Bundesministerium für Forschung und Technologie (BMFT) 1984: *Ethische und rechtliche Probleme der Anwendung zellbiologischer und gentechnischer Methoden am Menschen. Dokumentation eines Fachgesprächs im Bundesministerium für Forschung und Technologie*. Munich.

Bundesministerium für Jugend, Familie, Frauen und Gesundheit (BMJFFG) 1986: *Vierter Familienbericht. Die Situation der älteren Menschen in der Familie*. Bonn.

Bundesministerium für Jugend, Familie und Gesundheit (BMJFG) 1985: *Nichteheliche Lebensgemeinschaften*. Stuttgart: Kohlhammer.

References

Cherlin, Andrew J. 1992: *Marriage, Divorce, Remarriage*, rev. edn. Cambridge, Mass.: Harvard University Press.

Cherlin, Andrew J., and Furstenberg, Frank F., Jr 1986: *The New American Grandparent: a place in the family, a life apart*. New York: Basic Books.

Clarke, Angus 1994: 'Introduction'. In *Genetic Counselling: practice and principles*. London: Routledge, 1–28.

Coester-Waltjen, Dagmar 1994: 'Die Rollen von Mann und Frau im deutschen Familienrecht seit 1900'. In Venanz Schubert (ed.), *Frau und Mann. Geschlechterdifferenzierung in Natur und Menschenwelt*. Ottilien: Eos Verlag, 165–86.

Daele, Wolfgang van den 1985: *Mensch nach Mass? Ethische Probleme der Genmanipulation und Gentherapie*. Munich: Beck.

——1986: 'Technische Dynamik und gesellschaftliche Moral. Zur soziologischen Bedeutung der Gentechnologie'. *Soziale Welt*, 2–3, 149–72.

Davis, F. James 1991: *Who is Black? One nation's definition*. University Park, Pa.: Pennsylvania State University Press.

Diekmann, Andreas, and Engelhardt, Henriette 1995a: 'Die soziale Vererbung des Scheidungsrisikos. Eine empirische Untersuchung der Transmissionshypothese mit dem deutschen Familiensurvey'. *Zeitschrift für Soziologie*, 3, 215–18.

——1995b: 'Wird das Scheidungsrisiko vererbt?' *Informationsdient Soziale Indikatoren*, 4, 1–5.

Diewald, Martin 1993: 'Hilfebeziehungen und soziale Differenzierung im Alter'. *Kölner Zeitschrift für Soziologie und Sozialpsychologie*, 4, 731–54.

Dorbritz, Jürgen 1993–4: 'Bericht 1994 über die demographische Lage in Deutschland'. *Zeitschrift für Bevölkerungswissenschaft*, 4, 393–473.

Dorbritz, Jürgen, and Gärtner, Karla 1999: 'Berechnungen zur Kinderlosigkeit am Bundesinstitut für Bevölkerungsforschung'. *BiB-Mitteilungen (Informationen aus dem Bundesinstitut für Bevölkerungsforschung am Statistischen Bundesamt)*, 2, 13–15.

Dunkel, Wolfgang 1993: 'Alternpflege – und der Rest des Lebens. Bericht über eine empirische Untersuchung von Altenpflegekräften'. Manuscript, Sonderforschungsbereich 333 der Universität München, Munich.

Elschenbroich, Donata 1988: 'Eine Familie – Zwei Kulturen'. In Deutsches Jugendinstitut (ed), *Wie geht's der Familie?* Munich: Kösel, 363–70.

References

Emmerling, Dieter 1999: 'Ehescheidungen 1997'. *Wirtschaft und Statistik*, 1, 39–45.

Erler, Gisela, Jaeckel, Monika, Pettinger, Rudolf, and Sass, Jürgen 1988a: *Kind? Beruf? Oder beides? Eine repräsentative Studie über die Lebenssituation und Lebensplanung junger Paare zwischen 18 und 33 Jahren in der Bundersrepublik Deutschland im Auftrag der Zeitschrift Brigitte*. Hamburg: *Brigitte*.

—— 1988b: 'Männerwelten – Frauenwelten oder: Wer hat es besser?' *DJI-Bulletin*, 10.

Field, Martha A. 1988: *Surrogate Motherhood: the legal and human issues*. Cambridge, Mass: Harvard University Press.

Flitner, Andreas 1982: *Konrad, sprach die Frau Mama… Über Erziehung und Nicht-Erziehung*. Berlin: Severin und Siedler.

Franks, Suzanne 1999: *Having None of It: women, men and the future of work*. London: Granta Books.

Frevert, Ute 1985: ' "Fürsorgliche Belagerung": Hygienebewegung und Arbeiterfrauen im 19. und frühen 20. Jahrhundert'. *Geschichte und Gesellschaft*, 4, 420–46.

—— 1996: 'Die alte Unübersichtlichkeit. Familie im Wandel'. Manuscript, Konstanz.

Fthenakis, Wassilios E. 1995: 'Kindliche Reaktionen auf Trennung und Scheidung'. *Familiendynamik*, 2, 127–54.

Fuchs, Renate, Barbian, Elke, and Berg, Giselind 1994: 'Die Technisierung der Fortpflanzung. Zum Stand der In-vitro-Fertilisation in der BRD. Abschlussbericht an die Deutsche Forschungsgemeinschaft', hectograph copy, Berlin.

Furstenberg, Frank F. 1989: 'One Hundred Years of Change in the American Family'. In Harold J. Bershady (ed.), *Social Class and Democratic Leadership: essays in honor of E. Digby Baltzell*. Philadelphia, Pa.: University of Pennsylvania Press.

Furstenberg, Frank F., and Cherlin, Andrew J. 1991: *Divided Families: what happens to children when parents part*. Cambridge, Mass.: Harvard University Press.

Gates, Henry Louis 1995: *Coloured People*. London: Penguin.

Geissler, Birgit, and Oechsle, Mechthild 1994: 'Lebensplanung als Konstruktion'. In Ulrich Beck and Elisabeth Beck-Gernsheim, *Riskante Freiheiten. Zur Individualisierung von Lebensformen in der Moderne*. Frankfurt: Suhrkamp, 139–67.

Geyer, Michael 1995: ' "Sie nehmen die Kälte nicht wahr". "Westdeutsche" aus der Sicht eines "Ostdeutschen" '. In Elmar Brähler and Hans-Jürgen Wirth (eds), *Entsolidarisierung. Die Westdeutschen am Vorabend der Wende und danach*. Opladen: Westdeutscher Verlag, 217–37.

Giddens, Anthony 1991: *Modernity and Self-Identity: self and society in the late modern age*. Cambridge: Polity.

Giddens, Anthony 1994a: *Beyond Left and Right*. Cambridge: Polity.

Giddens, Anthony 1994b: 'Living in a post-traditional society'. In Ulrich Beck, Anthony Giddens, and Scott Lash, *Reflexive Modernization*. Cambridge: Polity, 56–109.

Giddens, Anthony 1997: *Sociology*, 3rd edn. Cambridge: Polity.

Giddens, Anthony 1998: *The Third Way: the renewal of social democracy*. Cambridge: Polity.

Goodman, Ellen 1995: 'A perpetual rush hour for baby boomers'. *International Herald Tribune*, 14 September.

—— 1996: 'How time and the lilacs go by so very quickly'. *International Herald Tribune*, 25 June.

Gross, Leonard 1983: *Versteckt. Wie Juden in Berlin die Nazi-Zeit überlebten*. Reinbek: Rowohlt.

Habermas, Jürgen 1992: *Faktizität und Geltung*. Frankfurt: Suhrkamp.

—— 1996: *Between Facts and Norms: contributions to a discourse theory of law and democracy*. Cambridge: Polity.

Hall, David R. 1996: 'Marriage as a pure relationship: exploring the link between premarital cohabitation and divorce in Canada'. *Journal of Comparative Family Studies*, 1, 1–11.

Hallson, Fridrik 1996: 'Lebensweltliche Ordnung in der Metropole'. In Wilhelm Heitmeyer and Rainer Dollase (eds), *Die bedrängte Toleranz*. Frankfurt: Suhrkamp, 271–312.

Hammes, Winfried 1996: 'Ehescheidungen 1995'. *Wirtschaft und Statistik*, 12, 770–6.

Hardach-Pinke, Irene 1988: *Interkulturelle Lebenswelten. Deutsch-japanische Ehen in Japan*. Frankfurt: Campus.

Haslinger, Alois 1982: 'Uneheliche Geburten in Österreich. Historische und regionale Muster'. *Demographische Informationen 1982*, 2–33.

Häussler, Monika 1983: 'Von der Enthaltsamkeit zur verantwortungsbewussten Fortpflanzung. Über den unaufhaltsamen Aufstieg der Empfängnisverhütung und seine Folgen'. In Monika Häussler, Cornelia Helfferich, Gabriele Walterspiel and Angelika Wetterer, *Bauchlandungen. Abtreibung – Sexualität – Kinderwunsch*. Munich: Frauenbuchverlag, 58–73.

Hecht, Ingeborg 1984: *Als unsichtbare Mauern wuchsen. Eine deutsche Familie unter den Nürnberger Rassengesetzen*. Hamburg: Hoffmann & Campe.

References

Heine-Wiedemann, Dagmar, and Ackermann, Lea 1992: *Umfeld und Ausmass des Menschenhandels mit ausländischen Mädchen und Frauen*. Schriftenreihe des Bundesministers für Frauen und Jugend, vol. 8. Stuttgart: Kohlhammer.

Heller, Agnes 1994: 'Die Zerstörung der Privatsphäre durch die Zivilgesellschaft'. *Ästhetik und Kommunikation*, 85–6, May, 23–35.

Hennen, Leonhard, Petermann, Thomas, and Schmitt, Joachim 1996: *Genetische Diagnostik – Chancen und Risiken. Der Bericht des Büros für Technikfolgen-Abschätzung zur Genomanalyse*. Berlin: Edition Sigma.

Hepp, Hermann 1994: 'Ethische Probleme am Anfang des Lebens'. In Ludger Honnefelder and Günter Rager (eds), *Ärztliches Urteilen und Handeln. Zur Grundlegung einer medizinischer Ethik*. Frankfurt: Insel, 237–83.

Hermann, Helga 1995: 'Ausländische Jugendliche in Ausbildung und Beruf'. *Aus Politik und Zeitgeschichte* 35, 23–9.

Hesse, Hans Albrecht 1994: *Der Schutzstaat. Rechtssoziologische Skizzen in dunkler Zeit*. Baden-Baden: Nomos.

Heuermann, Paul 1994: 'Verfassungsrechtliche Probleme der Schwangerschaft einer hirntoten Frau'. *Juristenzeitung*, 3, 133–9.

Hildebrandt, Karin, and Wittmann, Svendy 1996: 'Lebensziel Kinder?' *Die Frau in unserer Zeit*, 4, 35–41.

Hochschild, Arlie, and Machung, Anne 1989: *The Second Shift: working parents and the revolution at home*. New York: Viking Press.

Hoffmann-Riem, Christa 1988: 'Chancen und Risiken der gentechnologisch erweiterten pränatalen Diagnostik. Eine qualitative Studie bei Klienten humangenetischer Beratungsstellen'. Manuscript. Hamburg.

Hradil, Stefan 1995a: *Die 'Single' – Gesellschaft*. Munich: Beck.

—— 1995b: 'Die Sozialstruktur Deutschlands im europäischen und internationalen Vergleich'. In Bernhard Schäfers (ed.), *Gesellschaftlicher Wandel in Deutschland*, 6th edn. Stuttgart: Enke, 286–321.

—— 1996: 'Überholen ohne Einzuholen? Chancen subjektiver Modernisierung in Ostdeutschland'. In J. Kollmorgen et al. (eds), *Sozialer Wandel und Akteure in Ostdeutschland*. Opladen: Westdeutscher Verlag, 55–79.

Imhof, Arthur E. 1988: *Reife des Lebens. Gedanken eines Historikers zum längeren Dasein*. Munich: Beck.

Iyer, Pico 1993: 'The empire writes back'. *Time*, 8 February, 50–5.

Jochheim, Gernot 1993: *Frauenprotest in der Rosenstrasse*. Berlin: Edition Hentrich.

References

Jopt, Uwe 1997: 'Scheidungskinder – Problemkinder?' *Pädagogik*, 7–8, 16–20.

Kaufmann, Franz-Xaver, 1984: 'Familienentwicklung in Nordrhein-Westfalen'. *IBS-Materialien*, 17. University of Bielefeld.

Kaufmann, Franz-Xaver, Quitmann, J., Schulz, M., Simm, R., and Strohmeier, K. P. 1988: 'Familie und Modernität'. In Kurt Lüscher, Franz Schultheis and Michael Wehrspaun (eds), *Die 'postmoderne' Familie*. Konstanz: Universitätsverlag Konstanz, 391–415.

—— 1995: *Zukunft der Familie im vereinten Deutschland*. Munich: Beck.

Kentenich, Heribert et al. 1987: 'Am schlimmsten ist das Warten. Wie Paare die Invitro-Fertilisation erleben'. *Sexualmedizin*, 16, 364–70.

Kleiber, Lore, and Gömusay, Eva-Maria 1990: *Fremdgängerinnen. Zur Geschichte binationaler Ehen in Berlin von der Weimarer Republik bis in die Anfänge der Bundesrepublik*. Bremen: Edition CON.

Kohli, Martin 1986: 'Gesellschaftszeit und Lebenszeit. Der Lebenslauf im Strukturwandel der Moderne'. In Johannes Berger (ed.), *Die Moderne – Kontinuitäten und Zäsuren*. Special issue, *Soziale Welt*, 4. Göttingen, 183–208.

Kureishi, Hanif 1990: *The Buddha of Suburbia*. London: Faber & Faber.

Kytir, Josef, and Münz, Rainer 1991: 'Wer pflegt uns im Alter? Lebensformen, Betreuungssituation und soziale Integration älterer Menschen in Österreich'. *Zeitschrift für Sozialisationsforschung und Erziehungssoziologie*, 4, 332–54.

Lasch, Christopher 1977: *Haven in a Heartless World: the family besieged*. New York: Basic Books.

Leibfried, Stephan, Leisering, Lutz, Buhr, Petra, Ludwig, Monika, Mädje, Eva, Olk, Thomas, Voges, Wolfgang, and Zwick, Michael 1995: *Zeit der Armut. Lebensläufe im Sozialstaat*. Frankfurt: Suhrkamp.

Leigh, Wendy 1985: 'How to make sure you're going to live happily ever after – before you get married'. *New Woman*, July, 44–7.

Lenz, Ilse, Ramil-Weiss, Norma, and Thiemann, Heidi 1993: *Internationaler Frauenhandel. Eine Untersuchung über Prostitution und Heiratshandel in Nordrhein-Westfalen*. Dusseldorf: Ministerium für die Gleichstellung von Frau und Mann des Landes Nordrhein-Westfalen.

Liebau, Eckart 1996: 'Die Drei-Generation-Familie'. In Eckart Liebau and Christoph Wulf (eds), *Generation. Versuche über eine pädagogisch-anthropologische Grundbedingung*. Weinheim: Deutscher Studienverlag, 13–23.

References

Lucke, Doris 1990: *Rechtsratgeber Frauen*. Reinbek: Rowohlt.

McNally, Ruth 1995: 'Eugenics here and now'. *The Genetic Engineer and Biotechnologist* 15, 2–3, 135–44.

Makowsky, Arno 1996: *Hausmann mit Tochter*. Munich and Zurich: Piper.

Mammey, Ulrich, and Schiener, Rolf 1996: 'Das BiB-Aussiedlerpanel – Methodische Überlegungen zur Represäntativität'. *Zeitschrift für Bevölkerungswissenschaft*, 2, 145–70.

Markl, Hubert 1989: 'Genetik und Ethik. Rede anlässlich der Verleihung des Arthur-Burkardt-Preises 1989'. Hectograph copy. Stuttgart, 26 April.

Mattenklott, Gert 1992: *Über Juden in Deutschland*. Frankfurt: Jüdischer Verlag.

Mayer, Karl Ulrich 1991: 'Soziale Ungleichheit und Lebensverläufe'. In Bernd Giesen and Claus Leggewie (eds), *Experiment Vereinigung*. Berlin: Rotbuch, 87–99.

Mayer, Karl Ulrich, and Müller, Walter 1989: 'Lebensverläufe im Wohlfahrtsstaat'. In Ansgar Weymann (ed.), *Handlungsspielräume. Untersuchungen zur Individualisierung und Institutionalisierung von Lebensläufen in der Moderne*. Stuttgart: Enke, 41–60.

Mecheril, Paul, and Teo, Thomas (eds), 1994: *Andere Deutsche. Zur Lebenssituation von Menschen multi-ethnischer und multi-kultureller Herkunft*. Berlin: Dietz.

Merton, Robert K. 1976: 'Intermarriage and the Social Structure'. In *Sociological Ambivalence and Other Essays*. New York: Free Press, 217–50.

Merz, B. 1987: 'Matchmaking scheme solves Tay–Sachs problem'. *Journal of the American Medical Association*, 258, 2636–9.

Metz-Göckel, Sigrid, and Müller, Ursula 1985: *Der Mann. Eine repräsentative Untersuchung über die Lebenssituation und das Frauenbild 20–50-jähriger Männer im Auftrag der Zeitschrift Brigitte*. Hamburg: Brigitte.

Müller-Neumann, Markus, and Langenbucher, Heike 1991: 'Gentechnik und Humangenetik'. *Aus Politik und Zeitgeschichte*, 6, 1 February, 3–11.

Napp-Peters, Anneke 1995: *Familien nach der Scheidung*. Munich: Kunstmann.

Nave-Herz, Rosemarie 1992: 'Die Pluralität von Familienformen. Ideologie oder Realität'. *Familie und Recht*, 2, 186–91.

Neckel, Sighard 1997: 'Die ethnische Konkurrenz im das Gleiche. Erfahrungen aus den USA'. In Wilhelm Heitmeyer (ed.), *Was hält die Gesellschaft zusammen?* Frankfurt: Suhrkamp, 255–75.

References

Nippert, Irmgard, and Horst, Jürgen 1994: *Die Anwendungsproblematik der pränatalen Diagnose aus der Sicht von Beratenen und Beratern – unter besonderer Berücksichtigung der derzeitigen und zukünftig möglichen Nutzung genetischer Tests. Gutachten im Auftrag des Büros für Technikfolgen-Abschätzung beim Deutschen Bundestag.* Bonn: Deutsche Bundestag.

Nunner-Winkler, Gertrud 1989: 'Identität im Lebenslauf'. *Psychologie heute, Das Ich im Lebenslauf.* Weinheim: Beltz, 82–106.

Nuscheler, Frank 1995: *Internationale Migration. Flucht und Asyl.* Opladen: Leske & Budrich.

Oguntoye, Katharina, Opitz, May, and Schultz, Dagmar (eds) 1992: *Farbe bekennen. Afro-deutsche Frauen auf den Spuren ihrer Geschichte.* Frankfurt: Fischer.

Osterland, Martin 1991: '"Normalbiographie" und "Normalarbeitsverhältnis"'. In Peter A. Berger and Stefan Hradil (eds), *Lebenslagen, Lebensläufe, Lebensstile.* Göttingen: Schwartz, 351–62.

Ostner, Ilona 1992: 'Zum letzten Male. Anmerkungen zum "weiblichen Arbeitsvermögen"'. In Gertrude Krell and Margit Osterloh (eds), *Personalpolitik aus der Sicht von Frauen.* Munich: Hampp, 107–22.

Ostner, Ilona, and Boy, Peter 1991: 'Späte Heirat – Ergebnis biographisch unterschiedlicher Erfahrungen mit "cash" und "care"? Projektantrag an die DFG'. Bremen Xerox copy.

Pander, Hans-Jürgen, Artlich, Andreas, and Schwinger, Eberhard 1992: 'Heterozytogen-Testung bei Muskoviszidose. Eugenik, Prävention oder Instrument der humangenetischer Beratung'. *Deutsches Ärzteblatt*, 89, 51–2, 21 December, 2,786–90.

Parsons, Evelyn, and Bradley, Don 1994: 'Ethical issues in newborn screening for Duchenne muscular dystrophy: the question of informed consent'. In Angus Clarke (ed.), *Genetic Counselling: practice and principles.* London: Routledge, 95–112.

Pohl, Katharina, 1995: 'Kinderwunsch und Familienplanung in Ost- und Westdeutschland'. *Zeitschrift für Bevölkerungswissenschaft*, 20, 1, 67–100.

Pries, Ludger 1996: 'Transnationale Soziale Räume. Theoretisch-empirische Skizze am Beispiel der Arbeitswanderungen Mexiko-USA'. *Zeitschrift für Soziologie*, 6, 456–72.

Rabe-Kleberg, Ursula 1993: '"Zu Diensten!" – Über das Ende weiblicher Dienstbarkeit und die Zukunft der Sozial- und Pflegeberufe'. In Lutz Leisering, Birgit Geissler, Ulrich Mergner and Ursula Rabe-Kleberg (eds), *Moderne Lebensläufe im Wandel.* Weinheim: Deutscher Studienverlag, 129–41.

References

Reberg, Lotta 1997: *Mutters Freund und Vaters Frau. Familienleben nach der Trennung.* Reinbek: Rowohlt.

Reich, Günter 1991: 'Kinder in Scheidungskonflikten'. In Heiner Krabbe (ed.), *Scheidung ohne Richter. Neue Lösungen für Trennungskonflikte.* Reinbek: Rowohlt, 59–85.

Reich-Ranicki, Marcel 1993: *Über Ruhestörer. Juden in der deutschen Literatur.* Munich: Deutscher Taschenbuch Verlag.

Rerrich, Maria S. 1988: 'Kinder ja, aber – Was es Frauen schwer macht, sich über ihre Kinderwünsche klar zu werden'. In Deutsches Jugendinstitut, *Wie geht's der Familie? Ein Handbuch zur Situation der Familien heute.* Munich: Kösel, 59–66.

—— 1993: 'Gemeinsame Lebensführung. Wie Berufstätige einen Alltag mit ihren Familien herstellen'. In Karin Jurczyk and Maria S. Rerrich (eds), *Die Arbeit des Alltags.* Freiburg: Lambertus, 310–33.

Richards, Martin 1996: 'Family, kinship and genetics'. In Theresa Marteau and Martin Richards (eds), *The Troubled Helix: social and psychological implications of the new genetics.* Cambridge: Cambridge University Press, 249–74.

Ringen, Stein 1998: *The Family in Question.* London: Demos.

Ringler, Marianne 1994: 'Zur Schuldfrage in der psychosomatischen Betreuung bei pränataler Diagnostik'. In H. Kentenich, M. Rauchfuss and P. Diederichs (eds), *Psychosomatische Gynäkologie und Geburtshilfe 1993–1994.* Berlin: Springer, 106–13.

Rogge, Heinz 1965: 'Das Problem des Übertritts farbiger Amerikaner in die weisse Gesellschaft'. *Soziale Welt,* 2, 151–66.

Rosenblatt, Paul C., Karis, Terri A. and Powell, Richard D. 1995: *Multiracial Couples: black and white voices.* Thousand Oaks: Sage.

Rosenkranz, Doris, 1996: 'Folgen des familialen Wandels für die Pflege älterer Menschen. Familiendemographische Überlegungen'. In Hans Peter Buba and Norbert F. Schneider (eds), *Familie. Zwischen gesellschaftlicher Prägung und individuellen Design.* Opladen: Westdeutscher Verlag, 209–18.

Rosenstrauch, Hazel 1988: *Aus Nachbarn wurden Juden.* Berlin: Transit.

Roth, Philip 1992: *Patrimony: A True Story.* New York: Vintage.

Rothman, Barbara Katz 1988: *The Tentative Pregnancy: prenatal diagnosis and the future of motherhood.* London: Pandora.

Scheibler, Petra M. 1992: *Binationale Ehen. Zur Lebenssituation europäischer Paare in Deutschland.* Weinheim: Deutscher Studienverlag.

Schindele, Eva, 1990: *Gläserne Gebär-Mütter. Vorgeburtliche Diagnostik – Fluch oder Segen.* Frankfurt: Fischer.

References

Schmalz-Jacobsen, Cornelia, and Hansen, Georg (eds) 1997: *Kleines Lexikon der ethnischen Minderheiten in Deutschland*. Munich: Beck.

Schmid, Josef 1989: 'Die Bevölkerungsentwicklung in der Bundesrepublik Deutschland'. *Aus Politik und Zeitgeschichte*, 18, 28 April, 3–15.

Schmid, Werner 1988: 'Die Prävention des Down-Syndroms (Mongolismus)'. *Neue Zürcher Zeitung*, 20 January, 77.

Schmidt, Ulrich, Wolff, Gerhard, and Jung, Christine 1994: 'Verarbeitung des Schwangerschaftsabbruchs nach pathologischem Amniozentebefund: Schulderleben und Schuldgefühle'. In H. Kentenich, M. Rauchfuss and P. Diederichs (eds), *Psychosomatische Gynäkologie und Geburtshilfe 1993–1994*. Berlin: Springer, 158–68.

Schneider, Norbert F. 1995: 'Nichtkonventionelle Lebensformen – moderne Lebensformen?'. Lecture given at the 27th Sociology Congress in Halle, April, hectograph copy.

Schröter, Ursula, 1996: 'Ostdeutsche Frauen im "verfixten" siebenten Jahr'. *Die Frau in unserer Zeit*, 4, 22–8.

Schultz, Hans Jürgen (ed.) 1986: *Mein Judentum*. Munich: Deutscher Taschenbuch Verlag.

Schumacher, Jürgen 1981: 'Partnerwahl und Partnerbeziehung'. *Zeitschrift für Bevölkerungswissenschaft*, 4, 499–518.

Schwartz, Karl 1993–4: 'Kinder und Jugendliche in den Familien Alleinstehender in Deutschland im Jahr 1991'. *Zeitschrift für Bevölkerungswissenschaft*, 1, 71–91.

—— 1994: 'Kinderzahl deutscher Frauen 1992'. *BiB-Mitteilungen*, 1, 41–6.

Seidenspinner, Gerlinde, and Burger, Angelika 1982: *Mädchen '82. Eine Untersuchung im Auftrag der Zeitschrift 'Brigitte'*, report and tables. Hamburg: *Brigitte*.

Sommer, Bettina 1997: 'Eheschliessungen, Geburten und Sterbefälle 1995'. *Wirtschaft und Statistik*, 4, 220–5.

Spickard, Paul R. 1989: *Mixed Blood. Intermarriage and Ethnic Identity in Twentieth-Century America*. Madison, Wisc.: University of Wisconsin Press.

Stacey, Judith 1995: 'Der Kreuzzug der Revisionisten für Familienwerte in den USA'. In L. Christof Armbruster et al. (eds), *Neue Horizonte? Sozialwissenschaftliche Forschung über Geschlechter und Geschlechterverhältnisse*. Opladen: Leske & Budrich, 193–218.

Statistisches Bundesamt 1990: *Familien heute. Strukturen, Verläufe und Einstellungen*. Stuttgart: Metzler-Poeschel.

—— 1995a: *Im Blickpunkt: Ausländische Bevölkerung in Deutschland*. Stuttgart: Metzler-Poeschel.

—— 1995b: *Im Blickpunkt: Familien heute*. Stuttgart: Metzler-Poeschel.

—— 1997: *Emfänger/-innen von Erziehungsgeld und/oder Erziehungsurlaub. Zeitreihen 1987–1995*. Hectograph information sheet, March.

Stierlin, Helm 1995: 'Bindungsforschung: eine systematische Sicht'. *Familiendynamik*, 2, 206.

Stierlin, Helm, and Duss-von-Werdt, Josef 1995: 'Zu diesem Heft. Familie als Sozialisationsinstanz'. *Familiendynamik*, 2, 125–6.

Stolzfus, Nathan 1989: ' "Jemand war für mich da". Der Aufstand der Frauen in der Rosenstrasse'. *Die Zeit*, 30, 21 July, 9–13.

—— 1996: *Resistance of the Heart: intermarriage and the Rosenstrasse protest in Nazi Germany*. London: Norton.

Strümpel, Burkhard, Prenzel, Wolfgang, Scholz, Joachim, and Hoff, Andreas 1988: *Teilzeitarbeitende Männer und Hausmänner. Motive und Konsequenzen einer eingeschränkten Erwerbstätigkeit von Männern*. Berlin: Edition Sigma.

Teo, Thomas 1994: ' … "ich muss mich nicht entscheiden, ich bin beides … ". Zur Entwicklung und Sozialisation bi-/multirassischer Identität'. In A. Thomas (ed.), *Psychologie und multikulturelle Gesellschaft. Problemanalysen und problemlösungen*. Göttingen: Verlag für angewandte Psychologie, 82–93.

Testart, Jacques, 1988: *Das transparente Ei*. Frankfurt: Schweitzer.

Thränhardt, Dietrich 1995: 'Die Lebenslage der ausländischen Bevölkerung in der Bundesrepublik Deutschland'. *Aus Politik und Zeitgeschichte*, 35, 3–13.

Tizard, Barbara, and Phoenix, Ann 1995: *Black, White or Mixed Race? Race and racism in the lives of young people of mixed parentage*. London: Routledge.

Tölke, Angelika 1991: 'Partnerschaft und Eheschliessung – Wandlungstendenzen in den letzten fünf Jahrzehnten'. In Hans Bertram (ed.), *Die Familie in Westdeutschland*. Opladen: Leske & Budrich, 113–57.

Vaskovics, Laszlo A. 1991: 'Familie im Auflösungsprozess?'. In *Jahresbericht 1990*. Munich: Deutsches Jugendinstitut, 186–98.

—— 1994: 'Wiederentdeckung familialer Lebenswelten – ein Trend?' In Laszlo A. Vaskovics (ed.), *Familie. Soziologie familialer Lebenswelten. Soziologische Revue*, special issue 3, 4–17.

Vaskovics, Laszlo A., Buba, Hanspeter, and Rupp, Marina 1991: 'Die Partnerschaft in nichtehelichen Lebensgemeinschaften'. *Forschungsforum der Universität Bamberg*, 3, 36–43.

Vaskovics, Laszlo A., and Rupp, Marina 1995: *Partnerschaftskarrieren. Entwicklungspfade nichtehelicher Lebensgemeinschaften*. Opladen: Westdeutscher Verlag.

References

Walk, Joseph (ed). 1981: *Das Sonderrecht für die Juden im NS-Staat. Eine Sammlung der gesetzlichen Massnahmen und Richtlinien – Inhalt und Bedeutung. Mit Beiträgen von Robert M. Kempner und Adalbert Rükkert*. Heidelberg: D. F. Müller Juristischer Verlag.

Wallerstein, Judith, and Blakeslee, Sandra 1989: *Gewinner und Verlierer – Männer, Frauen, Kinder nach der Scheidung*. Munich: Droemer Knaur.

Walzer, Michael 1992: *Zivile Gesellschaft und amerikanische Demokratie*. Berlin: Rowohlt.

White, Walter 1969: *A Man Called White*. Salem, NH: Ayer Company Publishers.

Wilkinson, Helen 1998: 'The family way: navigating a third way in family policy'. In Ian Hargreaves and Ian Christie (eds), *Tomorrow's Politics: the third way and beyond*. London: Demos, 111–25.

Wolff, Gerhard, and Jung, Christine 1994: 'Nichtdirektivität und Genetische Beratung'. *Medizinische Genetik*, 2, 195–204.

Wood-Harper, Janice, and Harris, John 1996: 'Ethics of human genome analysis: some virtues and vices'. In Theresa Marteau and Martin Richards (eds), *The Troubled Helix: social and psychological implications of the new human genetics*. Cambridge: Cambridge University Press, 274–94.

Zapf, Wolfgang 1994: 'Staat, Sicherheit und Individualisierung'. In Ulrich Beck and Elisabeth Beck-Gernsheim (eds), *Riskante Freiheiten. Individualisierung in modernen Gesellschaften*. Frankfurt: Suhrkamp, 296–304.

Zwischenbericht der Enquete-Kommission Demographischer Wandel. Herausforderungen unserer älter werdenden Gesellschaft an den einzelnen und die Politik 1994: Bonn: Deutsche Bundestag.

Index

Note: page references in *italics* indicate tables and figures.

Index

Index

insemination, artificial 3, 7, 9
investment, marital 26–7, 140 n.5
Iyer, Pico 136

Jews, under National Socialism
    112–19, 121–2
Jochheim, Gernot 146 n.25
Jopt, Uwe 141 n.8a

Kafka, Franz 135–6
Kant, Immanuel 88, 93
Kaufmann, Franz-Xaver 53, 72, 83,
    90
Kentenich, Heribert et al. 94
kinship
    ascriptive 35, 45
    elective 35
Kleiber, Lore and Gömusay,
    Eva-Maria 119
Knopf, Michael 145 n.20
knowledge, expert 46–8, 62, 101,
    103
Kohlhaas, Irene 145 n.13
Kohli, Martin 45
Kureishi, Hanif 125
Kytir, Josef and Münz, Rainer 77, 80

labour market
    deregulation xi–xii
    and the family xi
    flexibilization xi–xii, 40
    and individualization x–xi, 44
    see also employment
Lasch, Christopher 1
law
    and divorce 24
    and family name 4–5
    and inheritance 7, 13–14
leave, parental 67
Leibau, Eckart 75
Leibfried, Stephan et al. 40
Leigh, Wendy 49
Lenz, Ilse et al. 129
life
    and decision-making 57, 58–61,
    62–3
    as planning project 42–63
life expectancy 75, 76
life politics 60–1

lifestyles
    and care in old age 77
    and choice 21–2, 97
    new 2–3, 6–7, 10, 15, 19, 40
love, and marriage ix
loyalty
    and divorce 32–3
    in succession family 37, 38–9
Lucke, Doris 32

McNally, Ruth 143 n.4
maintenance payments 31–2
Makowsky, Arno 142 n.2
Markl, Hubert 55, 143 n.3
marriage
    age at 50, *51*
    bicultural 105, 124, 133–5
    binational 9, 129–31, 133–5
    and cohabitation 2
    justification of 24–5
    lifelong ix, 12, 13, 19, 49
    preparation sessions 49
    racially mixed 107–8, 109, 112,
    113–15, 119–20, 124, 133, 137
    rates of xi
    and reproductive technology 7
    and romantic love ix
    successive 10–11, 33–9
    'trial' 27, 50, 52
    'weekend' 9, 10
    see also divorce
marriage contracts 49, 51–2
marriage market, international
    129–30
Marteau, Theresa 103
Mattenklott, Gert 121–2
Mayer, Karl Ulrich 141 n.3
Mecheril, Paul and Teo,
    Thomas 128
medicine
    and decision-making 58–61, 62–3
    and health of children 87, 89
medicine, reproductive ix, 59, 90–1
    and consent 59
    and genetic testing 54–8, 86,
    90–7
    and parenthood 3–4, 7, 9, 54–8,
    86–7, 97–102
    and sexuality ix

166

Compiled by Meg Davies (Registered Indexer, Society of Indexers)